No Such Thing as a *Pretty Good* Alligator Wrestler

Kids, Politics, and Family – Why Daddy Drinks

by Ron Hart

Schroder Media

Schroder Media

Published by Schroder Media LLC
2114 McKinley Road
Atlanta, Georgia 30318
www.schrodermedia.com

Managing editor: Jackie Hart
Cover + book design: Heidi Rizzi
Cartoonists: Michael Ramirez, Ed Hart, Paul Michael Holliday
Publisher and production editor: Jan Butsch Schroder
Proofreader: Michelle Covert

ISBN: 978-0-9762288-4-4
First printing, 2010

To Jackie

with love and thanks for all you do.

I know I don't say it enough, so next time
I don't say it, just pick up this book
and read it again.

Table of Contentions

Family, Friends, and Football

Why Daddy Drinks

Pre-ramble

By Ron Hart

In today's political landscape, an onlooker could be forgiven for wondering where conservative political satire writers are. Absent my hero P.J. O'Rourke, there are few non-leftist writers of political humor, leaving the important opinion and editorial field the sole dominion of the left.

So about six years ago I confronted my life-long struggle with literacy and, with both the encouragement of family and friends (who, through their attorneys, have demanded not to be identified) and with the miracle of spell check, I started writing a column for my hometown paper. To my surprise, the column is now carried in newspapers from Florida to California.

My intent is to educate, with humor and common sense, on the vital role capitalism, limited government, entrepreneurs, and free-markets play

True Blues by Andy Thomas, artist, www.andythomas.com

in providing the abundance our great nation has enjoyed. We are becoming a nation that boos the winners, especially in business. We cheer the underdog and denigrate achievers, with a sense of envy toward those who succeed.

I grew up, as my football coaches often remarked, "very very white," in the diverse small town of Columbia, Tennessee. Being the son of a policeman makes my pro-capitalism views more genuine than those espoused by trust fund kids like George Bush, Steve Forbes, or Al Gore.

Politics has always fascinated me, with each election pitting the Republicans against the Democrats to decide the direction of America. Would we become, as the GOP envisions, a nation of gun-toting white males, staying up at night worried that gays might marry, raping the earth for worldly gain while trying to codify their uncompromising interpretation the Bible into law?

Or would we fall subject to the rule of the Democrats' compassionate communist dream of a flamboyantly gay army in powder blue helmets, sashaying to the orders of third-world socialists whose country does not even have cable TV or an *American Idol* competition? An America that allows

Grand Ol' Gang by Andy Thomas, artist, www.andythomas.com

flag-burning, but only if done in an environmentally responsible way, that has a secular, lemming citizenry intent on living off of the Nanny Pelosi state of government cheese plates, and where the most insignificant slight is seen as a cause to riot and take a flat screen TV from greedy capitalists stupid enough to open a store in their self-blighted neighborhood?

The key for members of both sides is to have an ideology and go to great lengths not to put forth any real ideas to that end. We know them as politicians. It is a career that failed lawyers, successful car salesmen, and sundry scallywags can do that keeps them mercifully out of polite and productive society. It would work if only they were not compelled to make so many laws while in office.

A failed Bush administration ushered in the undefined political rhetoric of Obama's "Hope." Hope, which is not a strategy but a battle cry, fuels this administration. Hope also fuels the gambling and the online dating industries.

Given the hardened views and shrill discourse of our two entrenched political parties, I set out to find some area of reason between the two of them — which made me a Libertarian. And, as it turns out, many more are too but they just do not know it yet. We Libertarians tend to reside uncomfortably within the GOP, but have about as much power as the Log Cabin Republicans and not nearly the quality of Oscar parties.

So I set out to explain the Libertarian approach to issues with irreverent humor on a level that most potential recruits could understand. It was either the great philosopher Horace in 65 BC, or perhaps Sinbad, who once said, "What stops a man who can laugh from speaking the truth?" Humor, I found, given that it is so rare, increases the entertainment value of op-ed pieces and thus reaches a broader audience.

I am not a journalist. If I were then I could spell, construct cognitive sentences, and wake up every day trying to advance the liberal Obama agenda. I subscribe to what P.J. O'Rourke said in *Parliament of Whores* about his writing, "Humor, by its very nature, is more truthful than factual." Included in this book are some columns about the freakish side-shows of life; we know them as celebrities, who seem to want to opine on all things liberal. As Winston Churchill once said of a dog that performed for him by walking on its back two legs, "It is not that he does not do it well, it is that he does it at all."

There is also a section on the problems we bring upon ourselves that make life worth living: kids. Kids ground us and make us complete. They make us value the simple things — like being left alone.

The proceeds of this book go to my foundation, which seeks to give kids from lower-to-middle class backgrounds a chance to realize the American Dream. Those who work hard, start a business, hire others, and pay taxes to support their community are much better Americans than those conditioned by government schools to "raise awareness on social issues," become activists or otherwise complain and try to get something for free from others. Not that my heart does not go out to inner-city kids, especially those unable to dance their way out. We just feel that the possibility of being an entrepreneur is not presented to them as a viable alternative.

With that, this book offers you a nice respite from worthwhile reading. Even if you do not read it, just carrying the book will give the appearance of intellect and humor. This book is a perfect home companion for your weekend Sitz baths, right up until someone walks in on you — then it will be a jump ball as to which activity you are more embarrassed about.

P.J. O'Rourke and Ron Hart

Foreword

Hart to Hart

A View of Ron from Jensen, Jeb, and Hollis Hart

(from left) Hollis, Jackie, Ron, Jensen, and Jeb Hart

With my father, "meeting the parents" has added meaning. While many girls worry that their fathers will intimidate their boyfriends, I know for a fact that my father will make fun of mine. It is usually relentless, often to their faces, and always funny.

My father has the type of rare humor that is two parts wit, one part backwoods Tennessee, and one part Wall Street, all stirred with a healthy dose of reality. He doesn't so much tell jokes as he just has a hilarious way of looking at the world, a fact that became even more evident in compiling his articles for this book.

My brother, sister, and I are fortunate to have been raised in my father's household of humor. It has colored our lives immensely. In your hands you're holding the most amusing take on current events that you can get hold of today. As you read it, I hope you get to experience just a little slice of what life is like in our family – it's something everyone should get to enjoy at some point!

– *Jensen Hart*
  Vanderbilt 2010

Oct.1,1996

Dear Dad,

I am writing a petition for a Laptop. computer I admit that I don't need it, but I want it. I want a laptop computer because I want to be an author when I grow up and I figure if I want to be an author I need to pratice. Also for school for Home work and class work. All my life I wanted to be famous for some thing an author is what.

gensenHart

When I was asked to write a foreword for my father many questions came to mind. What would I say, how should I say it, how long should it be? But the most burning question that rattled around in my head was: who in their right mind let my father write a book?

My dad has an intriguing life story, one that is layered with subtle intricacies that make all the difference in why he turned out the way he did. But I am not going to divulge any of that background because that requires research, probably even a notepad, and might involve me engaging in actual journalism, a profession that I, like my father, wish to avoid at all costs.

So I'll just tell you what I know about my dad. He has always believed in the power of one's actions. When I was a kid, I played baseball like every American boy since Washington chopped down that cherry tree to make a Louisville Slugger. However, unlike every other American youth, I was the worst baseball player in the history of Buckhead Baseball, our local Little League organization.

I could not hit a ball to save my life. You might as well have told me to do a triple flip on skates. I was so slow I could not rustle leaves. After one game I went up to my dad, with my pants all muddy (not from sliding I assure you, but from picking clover in left field), and I told him that I had made an effort and that I just wasn't very good.

He said, "Son, don't ever mistake effort for success." As unsupportive as that statement may seem, I have never gotten a better piece of advice.

To believe in the power of self and one's ability to accomplish great things is one thing but to actually do it is a far greater challenge. Many people are comforted by the statement, "I tried my best," which is all well and good. But if you try your best then give up, what's the point? It takes effort to be successful, and it takes effort to maintain success.

My father is a lot of things, as you will see in his articles. He is a clever, insightful, and brilliant man. However, what is more difficult to transmit through print is how hard he has worked his whole life and how that has shaped him into the man whose columns you read in your newspaper, online, or in this book. So whether you like what he has to say or not, you had better respect him. I sure as hell do.

– *Jeb Hart*
University of Memphis 2013

"Don't walk around broke," was the advice Ron gave to his daughter the first time he discovered his four-year-old had only Cheerios in her overall pockets. That daughter was me. It is his views of the world and his steady sense of reality that have raised me to be who I am today.

Although most kids get advice from their fathers, the advice I received and my upbringing have been radically different than most because of the original and hilarious thoughts and ideas my father has brought to my attention. Without him, I know that I would live life with a less comprehensive view of the world and surely a more serious view as well.

You now have in your hand a piece of my father's thoughts and opinions all rolled up into one. As a teenager, it is hard for me to grasp political events; however, no matter what age you are, you will find yourself flying through the pages of this book. Even though it is no replacement for a lifetime of his humor and intellect, I hope you enjoy his book as much as I enjoy him as a father.

– Hollis Hart
The Westminster Schools 2010

Politics

*"Every government interference in the economy
consists of giving an unearned benefit, extorted by
force, to some men at the expense of others."*

— Ayn Rand

Note to Liberal Media: Give Bush a Break

"People who complain our press is biased should note that during World War II the press was on our side — and we won!"

— Cullen Hightower, American conservative
and author of *Cullen Hightower's Wit Kit*

A recent Pew Trust poll told us what we already know: The major media in America are very liberal. They are out of touch with mainstream citizens and their reporting is agenda-driven. With the presidential election coming up, you need to be able to filter the real news and facts from the daily, spoon-fed, anti-Bush subtext the national media cough up.

No doubt President Bush has had a tough eight weeks with the war in Iraq, these hypocritical second-guessing hearings, and then (adding injury to insult) he falls off his mountain bike and skins his face. John Kerry, always the opportunist and condescending smart-aleck (which is why he will probably lose), is quoted upon hearing of the mishap, "I guess he took his training wheels off." At least Bush's wife did not have to buy him his bike.

While some of Bush's first-term decisions on spending, wars of "choice," and other Libertarian issues have concerned me, the press has been so hateful toward Bush that it is hard to sort unreality from reason in judging him. The major media are dying because of their lack of objectivity and their desire to use the news to achieve their agenda.

The Abu Ghraib prison mess is just that. A few low-ranking military people who, for the first and last time in their lives were in positions of power over someone, abused that power. But no one has ever died of humiliation — just ask Al Gore. The prison scandal, while embarrassing, is nothing compared with what went on in Iraq under Saddam Hussein or what will go on there if we leave. The left would call what happened at Abu Ghraib "torture." Cheney probably calls it a fraternity prank.

Torture, if you believe the left, can only be used by them to go after non-liberals in their papers. They would call unkind words that might hurt a terrorist's self-esteem torture; Bush would consider torture having to read an intelligence memo before going to war. I am sure Cheney and Secretary of Defense Donald Rumsfeld do not consider what we do with prisoners who are out to destroy our country as torture. They would probably call it "government-assisted Pilates."

The media have made us hypersensitive and always apologetic to the world. If the Clinton administration had broken down a few al-Qaeda detainees, we might have learned of the 9/11 plot. Our enemies only understand power and force. Nothing we do will make them hate us more. Folks, this thing ain't going to be settled by having a weekend diversity workshop or a "We Are The World" song sung by Bono and other stars.

Pure muscle is why Saddam Hussein was able to stay in power in Iraq. My guess is that we will look back on this and realize that Saddam's thugocracy was not a bad way to control that country, rather than spending American soldiers' lives and our national treasure and putting our children deeper into debt.

The last time America was attacked without provocation was by Japan. We dropped two atom bombs on them. That finally ended things, saved countless American and Japanese lives, and is viewed by history (since it was done by a Democrat) as a great move.

A buddy of mine pondered what it might have been like if the modern media were writing about Bush as president during World War II. Here are some headlines from that war, rewritten as they would appear today:

December 7, 1941
Then: "Japan Attacks Pearl Harbor"
Now: "Bush Administration Missed Signs of Obvious Japanese Attack: Senator Theodore Kennedy, D-Mass., Calls for Hearings"

December 11, 1941
Then: "Germany Declares War on United States"
Now: "Bush Fails to Negotiate a Peaceful Solution with European Power: Churchill and Bush Alienate Europe"

September 8, 1943
Then: "Italians Surrender to Germans"
Now: "Pearl Harbor Victim Families Fault Bush for Attack"

June 6, 1944
Then: "D-Day Invasion of Normandy Begins"
Now: "Rumsfeld Approves Risky Invasion Scheme; Many U.S. Soldiers Slaughtered"

August 6, 1945
Then: "Atomic Bomb Dropped on Hiroshima"
Now: "Bush Massacres Thousands of Innocent Japanese"

1945
Then: "U.S. Wins World War II"
Now: "American Citizens Threatened with Job Losses to Germany and Japan as War Ends"

1948
Then: "Marshall Plan Passed"
Now: "Halliburton to Get Contract to Help Rebuild Europe"

Right or wrong (and I think this war in Iraq was a mistake), when the media are so against a president and poison his every attempt to defend the country, our enemies, who get CNN in this worldwide, 24-hour satellite-TV world we live in, are emboldened. If we are in a war, I support our president and our troops and would do nothing to harm our efforts. We can sort out later among ourselves if going to war was a good idea. I personally think it will be a trillion-dollar social studies experiment that will fail. But I may be wrong.

When the liberal media portray stories the way they do, our enemies see us as weak and divided. They are made to feel they are winning and in the right. It breeds more suicide bombers and uprisings. It endangers our troops and emboldens our enemies. I ask the media to not editorialize, but just to do their jobs and, most importantly, to think beyond their endemic hatred for Bush. Fox News is trouncing CNN in the ratings, which tells us that middle America wants "fair and balanced" coverage. According to those ratings, we seem to be getting it from Fox.

In our 2004 election, sadly all we had to choose from on the opposition side were John Kerry, Howard Dean, Rev. Al Sharpton, the Ralph Nader of our generation Dennis Kucinich, and John Edwards. If I drew those five in a poker hand, I would fold immediately. *American Idol* produces a better quality and variety of contestants. John Kerry will be the nominee of this crowd. It will be like being Valedictorian of summer school.

The media will trick you into believing that John Kerry is the medicine this country needs now. Unless that medicine is Nyquil, don't fall for it. He has not articulated anything substantially different than Bush has on any matter of substance. Second guessing Bush is not a strategy.

Would I prefer another Republican as president who perfectly fits my Libertarian views? Probably, yes. I wish Bush would spend less, value the separation of church and state, and muzzle Ashcroft. I might even vote for a Libertarian candidate just to send a message. But, rest assured, Bush is not getting a fair shake from a rabid media bent on his demise.

We have an odd dynamic in our country. We have only two choices for our president, but we can choose from forty *American Idol* contestants. As trivial as it is, a higher percentage of the population votes on *American Idol*.

Although the press hasn't told you, both Kerry and Bush have fallen off a bike lately. I would like to live in an America where at least one of our two presidential candidates could actually ride a bike. I'd just feel better about things going forward.

"COME ON, WHO WANTS TO RIDE THIS IN 2012?"

Billion Here, Billion There

"The taxpayer is someone who works for
the government but does not have to take
a civil service examination."

— Ronald Reagan

It has long been said that money is the root of all evil. Yet it seems the government spends a good bit of time taking ours. So by that way of thinking they must be the most evil of all.

And as Richard Hatch — who won $1 million on the debut of *Survivor* — found out, if you do not pay the government, it will send you to prison. A judge said that Hatch lied repeatedly on the witness stand and failed to pay taxes on his huge prize. Hatch won *Survivor* by getting others voted off the island. In prison, he will have to work to get other prisoners voted off of him.

So with tax day looming, you have just one more week to avoid paying taxes by declaring yourself a televangelist, an Indian reservation, or an offshore corporation. Or better yet, get involved in a cash-only business like being a hooker. The government rewards that by not taxing them. In fact, the hookers are running a tax-day special — for an extra $25 they will handle your extension.

I have espoused the virtues of the "Fair Tax," which is a simple tax on all people in America and collected like a sales tax when we purchase something. At least Hatch clearly knew that he was not paying taxes on his money, but for most of us, the current tax code, which has been written by lobbyists over the years, is way too complex and very costly to comply with. It punishes success and seeks to comfort us in ways that cause us to lose sight of business objectives.

Our current tax system taxes virtue. It taxes us when we work hard, marry, donate, save, hire employees, and die. It encourages spending, debt, and write-offs. In short, it is a mess, and is something that one or both of the parties needs to address. There is so much support for tax reform and simplification that I am astounded neither party has seized upon it.

Recent attempts to repeal the "death tax" (estate tax) stalled. If they keep the same tax code I hope they change one thing: if a lobbyist buys a senator, he ought to have to show his receipt. The theory of taxes is that they are fair. But the least fair tax of all is the death tax, which taxes the most productive, altruistic, and frugal among us. And it does it twice, once when the person makes the money and then, after he saves the money and pays taxes on his investment, the government taxes the money again at 55 percent when he dies. Like all taxes, this takes capital from the most productive hands in society (entrepreneurs, business owners, savers, and capitalists) that employ people and pay even more taxes through their businesses, and redeploys it to the least productive part of our society; we know them as politicians.

Bush has weakened himself and the Republicans by not vetoing a spending bill — ever. Bush seems to have saved a good bit on his own personal taxes by completely writing off his second term. He lost his "veto-ginity" recently in a symbolic veto of federal funding for stem cell research, which shows just where his priorities are. So much for the first president with an MBA.

And, of course, Congress is no better in showing economic sensibility; our representatives are so proud of themselves that they voted themselves another raise recently, like they always do, late in the session and with a voice vote. Now before you get all mad at them, realize that when your congressman has money there is a "trickle down" effect that helps others when they spend that money. Hookers, DUI defense lawyers, and liquor stores really benefit. As Congress trickles down on us and tells us it is raining, it is comforting to know that our representatives will have a nice pay raise next year for their fine work.

And if you do not think the billions and billions of dollars of our money that Congress spends (and then borrows for the rest) is a lot of money, think of it this way. A billion seconds ago it was 1959. A billion minutes ago, Jesus was alive. A billion hours ago it was the Stone Age. And, a billion dollars is what Congress spends of our money *every eight hours*.

Bush and his cronies have been a bitter disappointment to me in the way they have spent money. Earmarks and pork still flow; now they just flow to GOP states, which does not make it any more right than when they went to blue states.

We really need to get spending and taxes under control. The less we give government the less it will probably spend.

Like the Democrats before them and most likely in 2008 when they win the presidency, politicians run to us breathlessly demanding money for the conjured-up imperative of the day. It's the big bad threat that they both create and say they protect us from — by spending our money of course. Like my dad told me when I moved to New York to work for Goldman Sachs, "Son, never buy a Rolex from a man in Times Square who is out of breath." So, too, it is with Congress; never let them jam a spending bill down our throats when they act as if it is of dire importance. It is how they hoodwink us. Always have and always will.

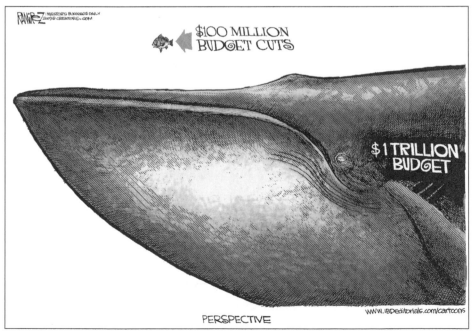

By permission of Michael Ramirez and Creators Syndicate, Inc.

Capitol Punishment

"The hardest thing in the world to understand is the income tax."

— Albert Einstein

Imagine — no IRS. Enjoy the thought! But in all reality this could happen if the new Fair Tax is passed. I know that George Bush, who is not "book smart" (and I question at times if he is even magazine smart), does not like to read much. I guess he is such a delegater that he married a librarian to do that. I am all but sure that they did not meet in a library.

But if he does read a book this summer, I hope it is Neal Boortz and Congressman John Linder's *New York Times* bestseller *The FairTax Book.* There is keen interest in this simple tax that abolishes the IRS and makes everyone, including illegal aliens, pay taxes.

Just to refresh you on how Washington works: when congress "gives us" something, in the form of a government program, it must first take money from us to do so. But as they take a dollar from us, they keep about 40 cents of it in D.C. to administer it, then they magnanimously and with great ceremony "give us money" in the form of a program that we don't usually need or that we never asked for. They then run it through donors' sticky fingers, which they like to call "government contracts." After patting themselves on the back, they head off to a drug company-sponsored boondoggle or to their office to fondle an intern.

Each politician who runs for office speaks of bringing accountability to Washington D.C., right up to the point he or she is elected. I have given up on accountability in D.C.; I would settle for an accountant just to tell me where all the money was spent.

Sadly, even the Republican Congress spends money like a drunken Kennedy. As a part of the Libertarian branch of the GOP, which is akin to being a Log Cabin Republican sans the cool Halloween parties these days as relates to our influence, this has been my greatest disappointment. Ted Stevens, R-Alaska, takes money for his state just as egregiously as Senator Robert Byrd did for West Virginia when the Democrats were in control. Ted Stevens represents the hubris that will be the downfall of the GOP. It is all about power and money.

Everyone is a big deal there when they are spending other people's money. They are like drunks at the bar buying drinks for everyone on your credit card. At least drunks are fun to watch. The congressmen make me sick to listen to. It must end, but I fear it will not.

Even Senator Hillary Clinton says she is fed up with the spending (mainly because she is going to run for president). She even said she might show up in the president's office unannounced to get some answers, which has historically been her best way of getting information.

Here is how the FairTax works: We all pay one rate of about 19 percent of just what we spend. There is no tax taken from our paychecks; you bring home 100 percent of what you make. We only pay tax when we buy something. That way those evil consumers who buy expensive things pay more taxes.

And since Wal-Mart and others collect sales tax now, we would just let them continue to do so for the whole country. If you choose to consume, then you pay tax. If you save, you do not.

Those obnoxious rich folks you are conditioned to hate have to pay $20,000 extra when they buy a big Mercedes. The many illegal aliens who currently escape the income tax system would have to pay their fair share too. Ditto for foreigners, drug dealers, and trust-fund babies. The tax will apply to lawyers' fees, doctors' fees, and accounting fees, which have been lobbied out of taxation. There are provisions for the poor to get monthly rebate checks as long as they are looking for a job.

I am a smart guy — just ask me — and I think one of my Nobel Prizes was for Economics. But I cannot and will not do my own taxes. I rely on my CPA entirely, as the tax laws are so complicated these days that they defy common sense. We have a tax code that is a compilation of years of Congress paying back certain groups for their donations and lobbying them. On the rare occasion that congress does rewrite the tax code, the main people at the table are the lobbyists for the various interests to be taxed. It is like having your cocaine dealer show up at your drug abuse intervention.

Our IRS regulations have 8,551,440 words; it takes the average person thirteen hours to do his tax return. We spend $193 billion annually to comply with the tax code. Al Gore and others said they "simplified the tax forms." In my view, they have "simplified" them beyond all comprehension.

I called the IRS once to get them to explain one of their "explanations" on an issue. If you think you don't understand the code, try talking to one of the idiots they have interpreting their own code. Yet they have a $10 billion budget and 104,900 employees — four times as many as the FBI.

Our tax code is an antiquated and contorted system that needs to be dismantled for simplicity's sake. It seeks to control the behavior of taxpayers with gimmicky deductions (like solar tax credits, or getting a big deduction if you buy a Toyota Prius), rather than to run an efficient government.

I did contemplate saving on taxes once by declaring myself an Indian reservation. My accountant said no, but that I could write off lunch with my friend Scott as entertainment. I said, "No way, you were not at lunch. There was nothing entertaining about it."

Success in America is rewarded with high taxes. Not only does Washington take a large part of our income, it spends more than it takes in and issues debt that our kids will have to pay.

To quote from The FairTax Book, "Our current tax system is one that punishes the behaviors Americans value and rewards behaviors we abhor. Those in our society who work hard and achieve are punished with taxes that approach confiscatory levels. Eschew hard work, and follow the path of least resistance, and your tax burden all but disappears while the taxpayer-funded government largesse pours in."

It is very hard for me to believe that our Founding Fathers, who formed this country to avoid high taxes, would recognize it today. We do not need to tinker with the tax code again — we need to abolish it.

Cut the Tab On Drunk Uncle Sam

"A man has to believe in something. I believe I'll have another drink."

— W.C. Fields

Our Washington government is starting to remind me of my drunk uncle. Perhaps we all have one. We called him our Druncle.

He is the guy who shows up late at family reunions, in a remorseful "going to make it up to us all" way, given that no one knows where he has been and what he has been doing for the year. Upon a late and drunk arrival, he wants to impress, so he starts to talk big to all the kids about how he is going to give them money — money that he does not have. Of course, all the adults at the reunion know all about this uncle's past false promises and that he has more liens on him than Michael Vick. He knows they know, so he has to ply his malarkey with the most vulnerable and those with unformed opinions of him: the simple-minded children. He is much like our government, which panders to the most gullible among us with its stimulus rebate money, which it then goes and borrows, adding to the $9 trillion debt.

My personal uncle smells like cheap store-bought gin that comes in plastic bottles, and he has the demeanor of a lookout for a cockfight. Yet he does, on occasion, impart wisdom to the underage kids. One year he told them, "In Budweiser there is wisdom, in bourbon there is freedom, and in water, there are bacteria." It cost all the parents money the next year, as the children demanded only bottled water thereafter.

The kids listen to him (the way we listen to politicians) because he differs from their parents in that he tells them only what they want to hear. He says they can live for now and not worry about the future. Further holding their attention is his track record: There is a 50-50 chance that he passes out — always a memorable experience for the kids. We call it "getting toe-up."

Some of my relatives say his drinking and womanizing are a disease. I think of it more as a lifestyle choice. Either way, it should serve as a warning to kids who contemplate starting drinking because they think life is great. I think my uncle drinks because he knows that it isn't.

We all have this sad uncle metaphor for our Congress: well past his usefulness, spending money that he does not have, making promises that he cannot fulfill, and clearly on the downward half of a very mediocre life. His sex life limited by age and the advent of commercially viable pepper spray, nothing but delusional nostalgia keeps him going, and the thought that someone might believe his good intentions.

Like my uncle the lush, the U.S. government also made dramatic pronouncements of its pandering intentions in the form of an IRS letter sent to all of us informing us of the impending rebate check. Our government spent $42 million of our money (well, not technically our money, as it was just borrowed in our name) to send out a self-congratulatory mailer that tells us of its impending "largesse."

This is the same pandering that Hillary Clinton did with her "gas tax holiday." Now, do not get me wrong. I am for any holiday that does not involve family or a long church service, but her thinly veiled attempt to garner votes from the most shortsighted among us was shameful.

I would not mind giving tax dollars to government to fund something it does well. To date, I have not been able to figure out what that is. While FedEx and UPS made money last year, the U.S. Postal Service (I always chuckle when they call themselves a "service") lost $2.2 billion. What makes this worse, was that most of the money was lost in the mail.

Sadly, the GOP, having been at the open bar of Washington for eight years now and having become drunk on its own delusions of power, is no better than the Democrats when it comes to stupid spending. Bush has been president since 2001 and has done nothing to curtail spending. The bureaucracy in D.C. seems to swell in attempts to meet the ever-expanding needs of the bureaucracy it supports. I wish we could cut Washington's bar tab off and make politicians sober up. But as long as they have an open tab on us, this insanity will continue.

No Pork Barrel Project Left Behind

"Without education we are in a horrible and deadly danger of taking educated people seriously."

— G.K. Chesterton, English essayist, novelist and critic

Finally, the kids are back in school and all is right with the world, at least at my house. We still have that ill-thought-out war thing in Iraq, but that seems minor compared to getting the children back into a school routine. I have long maintained the problem with kids is that you have to talk to them. After about three months of summer with them I appreciate the simple things in life, like when they are not around.

In a perfect world, kids would be sent away and returned when they are old enough to drink. That is why the rich have always preferred boarding schools. They are a place to store kids until they are old enough to see things your way. If they do not, that is what grad school is for.

Right now I can't even seem to agree with my son on even small things, like which direction his baseball cap should point. He maintains that it should point backward, and I asked him to examine the hat closely and perhaps read the manufacturer's specs on the hat. They apparently do not teach this at his school, as all the boys have their lids on backwards.

Frustrated with my boy, I have even threatened, when mad, to send him to a military school. And not a good one, either — one of those with pending investigations about treatment of students that has to advertise on bus benches. He remains unafraid.

Each new school year the government focuses on a certain theme. We all remember Nancy Reagan's "Just Say No" mantra when drugs were a problem. Thank goodness this concisely worded dictate came about when it did and completely eradicated drugs in the U.S. Then came: "Just say no to sex," which worked just as well. I say we come out with a "Just say no, to just saying no and start acting in your own enlightened self-interest."

Bill Clinton was intent on fighting obesity and led by example. In fact, he was so determined he would fight obesity that he did so every time — until she gave in. Bill disappointed more portly women than Jenny Craig. But in many ways, I miss him.

This year the theme is a focus on math, and that is a good thing. Just to look at "Hooked on Phonics" George Bush, you would not think that he would be good at math. And you would probably be right.

Politicians saying we need to learn math seems hypocritical. It always scares me when politicians make speeches that have estimated numbers, invariably in the billions of dollars (they seldom mess up small), and they just say the number.

The "Big Dig" in Boston that Ted Kennedy got us to pay for started off at a predicted cost of $2.5 billion, with a completion date of 1998. It is now $13.6 billion and not done yet. In 1991, when this was debated on the Senate floor, Sen. Ted Kennedy (D-Mass. and Chappaquiddick Swim Champion) said, and I am not making this up, "There is no intention of repeating or coming back for additional resources."

You look at the politician and you use history as a reference. You know deep down he has no idea if that number he just used in his speech is correct. And I really love it when politicians use a decimal point, when they predict, say, a $14.4 billion cost. The ".4" just shows they have a sense of humor or they really think you are more apt to believe them if they act precise.

Sadly, Bush and the Republicans are not much better. When Bush gives a speech he always slows down and says the projected number extra slowly, then smiles, as though he is very pleased with himself for reading it right. Bush gave a speech the other day on C-SPAN II (we political junkies call the channel "The Deuce"). In it he said it would cost $180.5 billion to remove all illegal aliens from the U.S. Ironically, and by my calculations, if we were to hire the illegal workers themselves to do it, the cost would be $3 billion.

My point is that it is important we and the politicians, who seem to love the blank check that we give them called taxation and deficit spending, really understand math before they are allowed to put dollar signs behind a government spending program.

The federal budget is more screwed up than Mike Tyson's checkbook. My guess is it can all be traced back to a poor math education or the fact that the money they spend is not theirs. This is the Congress that is taking the "security" out of Social Security. They continue to write checks that future generations cannot cover so they can live for the now.

Nancy Pelosi, whose face is starting to look like a cross between a Picasso and a ransom note, is a woman who knows how to spend someone else's money. Just ask her rich husband. She and the Democrats try to scare old people by saying they "stood up against those who would end Social Security." Thank you again, Nancy, for having the courage to stand up against something that no one has even suggested.

Given a trend of deteriorating math scores among our youth, it is good that ciphering is to be the focus this year. And it is about time. Nothing says math skills like a politician giving a populist speech about what he is going to give everyone from the Treasury.

I read somewhere that something like four out of three high school graduates don't fully understand fractions, and I find that embarrassing. I guess it is because math majors are not cool enough for kids to want to emulate them.

You would think that with the gazillionaires created in the high-tech world, such as math geek Bill Gates and those Google dudes, it might become cooler. They even made a recent movie about men really good at math. It's called *The 40 Year Old Virgin*.

Oh well, some things never change.

Less Government Is More

"Giving money and power to government is like giving whiskey and car keys to teenage boys."

— P. J. O'Rourke

I promised to propose a solution for the competing desires of the liberal Vermont Republic and conservative League of the South to secede from each other. Here are my ideas for what we really can do to make this work.

Let's face it: We live in a 51 percent versus 49 percent country. Each election is close, and we are split on how we want to run the ever-expanding federal government. Even as European countries like Great Britain and France become more conservative and pro-capitalist, we seem poised to elect a socialist Democrat who wants to expand the powers of Washington into health care and beyond. It will not work.

I held out hope in 1994, when the Republicans swept into a majority in Congress, and they did force a few good things such as welfare reform and lower taxes. But as it turns out, over time they preferred power over principle, and they have been a bitter disappointment.

In short, the federal government provides us with one important service: national defense. Indeed, to let us know how important they are, the feds often use our military in wars of choice that never seem to turn out well. In fact, it is no longer "defense." Rather, it is an offense that they take pleasure in deploying our troops. While confiscating 38 percent of our income in taxes to do so, Congress also runs up trillions in deficits because it has no collective sense.

I would not mind letting the federal government do the things it does best, if only I could determine just what these are.

The federal government seldom does anything that pleases locals, and is only about preservation of its powers. Realistically, one cannot move to another country if one does not like what the feds do — unless you are a movie star who threatens to do it if Bush is elected. Most don't follow through, which was a pity in the case of Barbra Streisand and Rosie O'Donnell.

The Hollywood liberals, even as California heads toward demise with its high taxes and regulations, support uber-liberal Barack Obama. They even had two fundraisers for him recently; one was a $25,000 a plate dinner, the other was $5,000. This reminds us that, even though the libs in Hollywood think the Republicans are elitist and the country should be made more socialist by the federal government, they never want to lose sight of the fact that there will always be an A-list and a B-list for them.

My solution to the unworkable yet appealing idea of secession is to devolve more powers to the states and fewer to Washington. It is what our Founding Fathers intended. And if you read the *Federalist Papers*, you will realize that they never intended our central government in Washington to be this expansive and overbearing. If California and New York want high taxes and residents are willing to pay, then so be it. If Texas, Tennessee, and Florida want no state income tax, then let's see who grows and who does not. My bet is on the low-tax states.

If you want an abortion, then move to a state that allows it. If you want to smoke weed, then go to California (their Obama inspired motto: "Yes We Cannabis"). If you think we should pay for everything a lazy welfare person demands, then go to a state that gives him flat-screen TVs and, instead of government cheese, offers an assortment of French cheeses that are both delicious and presented in a pleasing manner.

The basic reason that we fought for our independence is to do what we damn well please as long as it does not harm others. Yet at every turn, the federal government seems to want to make us do as it thinks we should, even if it comes down to using windmills, driving a Toyota Prius, or now, being forced to join the Hillary/Obama Health Care Plan.

The Dems who complain loudest about the inept response to Hurricane

Katrina are the ones advocating government's takeover of health care. And the Republicans, who ran on the theme that big government does not work and then once elected, set out to prove it, are no better. The Bush White House even had to defend a suit claiming the proposed anti-gay marriage amendment infringed on states' rights and sought to impose the president's religious agenda on the country. Bush has delayed his response while he decides if he can actually argue with that. If that amendment passes, my guess is that the religious right will ask Bush to outlaw dirty dancing next.

Our free-spending federal government thinks it is doing things well, and is filled with enough hubris to believe it should tell other countries what to do — it calls it foreign policy. The real answer is that less money and power need to be vested with Washington and more at the state level.

By permission of Michael Ramirez and Creators Syndicate, Inc

Headed Back to Bondage

Being Libertarians, we get to pick from the best of the Democratic and Republican parties. We usually make money like Republicans and have the sex lives of Democrats. And that is just one of the good things about being who we are.

When I have a deep talk these days with either a hardcore Democrat or rabid Republican, it always starts out with their "talking points," which they mechanically recite as if they are just going through the motions and trying to re-convince themselves of their beliefs. After the second bourbon or so, a bit of self-doubt comes through and they begin to question themselves and their party.

Democrats realize that they are a utopian theoretical party that is more about making people feel good — most importantly, themselves. They tax and vilify the most productive members of society and go through the motions of redistributing wealth. They are beholden to an odd collection of interests that most Americans do not like. Democrats line up their constituents by categories according to their perceived victimhood. Each class of "victims" wants some form of reparations for historic slights, both real and imagined; none of which happened to them directly, mind you. But they are there with their hand out looking to get something for nothing — always a noble endeavor.

The bad news for us is that liberal Democrats take money from the most productive part of society and, after they take their cut of graft and patronage out of it, distribute a fraction of it to its least productive members who usually cash their government checks at the liquor store. By doing so, they validate this part of society's lethargy and allow them to continue to wallow in their victimhood. The more they convince folks they are victims, the better voting bloc the Democrats have. Clearly, Democrats do not want people to succeed, because they then become Republicans.

After their third bourbon, Republicans will tell you that George Bush has set the party back twenty years. He did so by going against the very fundamental beliefs of the GOP: limited government, less spending, privacy, and individual rights. Bush has blurred the line between church and state, folding to the religious right faster than a cheap lawn chair. He has us in what can only be viewed as a religious war and it is increasingly apparent that he spun intelligence to get us in this mess. He also signed into law a non-market-driven prescription drug bill that is the second largest entitlement in history. Bush continues to disappoint me in ways I never imagined. He seems like he wants to hang on to his 32 percent approval ratings like it is a $500 a month rent-controlled apartment in the Upper East Side of Manhattan.

The traditional minimal government conservatives such as Barry Goldwater and Ronald Reagan have been replaced by a new breed of big government "compassionate conservatives" — entrenched Republicans who seek to use their power to reshape citizens' thinking toward their own religious and world views. They do not heed Goldwater's maxim that before any decision is made, legislators should consider whether they are "maximizing freedom."

As a result of the populist pandering of both parties, our country's future is at stake. If you look at other cultures and democracies in history, they tend to flourish up to the point where voters determine that they can elect leaders who will give them the most generous payouts from the public treasury. Voices of reason and economic sensibility do not get elected until it is too late.

The Soviet Union spent more than it could afford on defense and to achieve full employment in non-business endeavors. As a result, that empire crumbled. Every great civilization's life cycle appears to follow a similar trajectory. Alexander Tyler, a Scottish history professor at the University of Edinburgh, supposedly identified the process as follows: "From bondage to spiritual faith; from faith to courage from courage to liberty; from liberty to abundance from abundance to complacency; from complacency to apathy; from apathy to dependence; from dependence back into bondage."

Note that liberty leads to abundance. And liberty — the freedom of people to choose and do as they will — is what Libertarians stand for. We must not lose sight of that, and when our politicians want to take away our liberties under the guise of national security, "the greater good" or expediency, we must not allow it.

George Bush has spent $1 trillion in Iraq by invading a country not responsible for 9/11, spent money like the Democrats he campaigned against by never vetoing a spending bill, gave us the largest entitlement program since FDR in the Prescription Drug benefit, bestowed renewed powers to the Feds to snoop on us, and assured us of a Democrat winning the White House in 2008. For this, Jimmy Carter just gave him an honorary Carter-era Democrat membership card that entitles him to a 15 percent discount at any restaurant in Plains, Georgia

By permission of Michael Ramirez and Creators Syndicate, Inc.

G8 — It's Not Just for Breakfast Anymore

With his poll numbers at a new low and his administration on the ropes, George Bush took a page from the Bill Clinton playbook and went overseas to act like a president. Bush is so unpopular that I am not sure he still gets the window seat on Air Force One.

As you might expect, world leaders were glad to see Bush, and they asked if he brought our treasury's checkbook again. Bush, beaming from the fact that we finally got Paris Hilton and Martha Stewart behind bars, was happy to deflect questions about why we have not captured Osama bin Laden.

The G8 Summit, for those of us who are wondering what a vegetable juice has to do with international diplomacy, is where the rich industrial countries meet each year so protesters from Europe can get sprayed with water cannons. It is like Disneyland Paris's water rides, except that there are lots of people there. It gives the Europeans something to riot about in the off years of the World Cup. These poorly groomed young protesters, who owe their education to the business prowess of their parents and governments, show their appreciation by throwing rocks at the capitalist pigs. Then they spend the balance of their lives trying to pick up liberal chicks by telling them they once "raged against the machine" by protesting.

The G8 also allows for photo ops of the leaders standing next to each other, so each country can see who grew the most from the year before. Asia never fares too well here; short of Yao Ming retiring from the NBA and running for office, it probably never will. Yet, in an ironic twist, it takes the most pictures.

The eight countries invited know the pleasure of being asked to solve all the world's ills, for which, in some convoluted logic, they get blamed. So the G8, which is more public relations for politicians than anything substantive, is more like all the student body presidents of all the high schools meeting in Nashville for the weekend. It is truly democracy in action.

President Bush spoke at the G-8 Summit, and he praised the Italians and Germans for being our "great allies." He went on to say, "Except, of course, for anytime we've ever been to war, either against you or without you in Iraq."

Under a more "inclusive" democrat regime surfacing in America, the G8 might be enlarged to the G-20 so as not to hurt any country's feelings. Imagine Yemen's surprise when they get their invitation to join. It might also serve the U.S. well to expand to the G-20 because at this spending rate, we are not going to be in the top eight wealthiest countries for long.

This year, however, there were some exciting fireworks. It seems European politicians are no different than ours. They all love to scare us with trumped-up problems that can be fixed if we just spend our tax money on their cronies. This year's haute couture fashionable fret is global warming. It is a perfect BS problem created by and for corrupt politicians. They scare you with catastrophic predictions of global doom then extract money from you (that goes to them and their cronies) to fix the unquantifiable problem that never existed. Let me explain global warming to you. On a sunny day, take your shoes off and step in your grass, then step on your driveway. Repeat this until you understand why temperatures supposedly have gone up.

With all their brilliance, after they solve global warming and the conflicts in the Middle East, our politicians are going to set their sights on resolving one of the longer-standing conflicts — the roadrunner/coyote wars.

Vladimir Putin, the Russian president who lists as his hobbies poisoning rivals, fishing bare-chested and shutting down his country's free press, diverted the world's attention from his return to totalitarian government by bringing up the problem of greenhouse gas emissions. Now I am not sure that a man named Putin should be pointing or pulling any fingers on this issue. If I am not mistaken, the treaty signed in the 1983 accord called "Da Who Smelt it, Dealt It" fully addressed this issue.

Bush also got to see the pope and sit in his Popemobile. The pope, fresh back from telling Africans they should not use condoms, continued to send odd messages to the masses. Who better to enlighten you on sex than the celibate pope? And what better guy to say using protection is wrong than one riding in a bullet-proof glassed-in Popemobile? They discussed how the pontiff pimped his ride and the terrible poverty in Africa. And what better way to discuss poverty than in the pope's gold-encrusted, second floor library in the Vatican? It just makes the kids in Darfur feel like he is rooting for them.

U2's lead singer Bono was there, of course. He has made so much money that now he likes to go around the world and ask countries to forgive the debts that were usually run up by previous corrupt governments. I am almost certain he does not forgive the folks who owe him money on his own bond portfolio. Bush was excited to meet Bono, yet there was an awkward moment when "W" suggested that he get back with Cher.

The countries in the G8 got to join their club because while they represent only 14 percent of the world's population, they are responsible for 65 percent of the economic output. We are the ones who provide the jobs, feed the poor, and fight the wars to free citizens from tyrants, so it would be logical that we are hated. We Americans have helped eradicate apartheid-like separatism in the world, saving it only for our congressional districts.

I'm not sure how it came about that poor countries got to hold the G8 countries responsible for pollution, overpopulation, and sectarian strife, not to mention their tendency to treat women poorly and children worse. Can it really be that not one of their problems stems from their own inability to organize, implement basic human rights, and protect invested business capital? Of course, shiftlessness, ancient idiotic traditions, religious fanaticism, and corrupt government rule have no role, either.

It seems interesting that the rich countries, the ones full of "greedy capitalists and corrupt corporations," the ones with the money and intellect, are asked to help the socialist/communist/theocratic countries that do not have greedy capitalists. I wonder if the two are tied together. Maybe they ought to commission a study.

An Inconclusive Half-Truth: Al Gore is Thawing

"It ain't what you don't know that gets you into trouble. It is what you know for sure that just ain't so."

— Mark Twain

Politics are funny. Who would have thought five years ago that Arnold Schwarzenegger would be governing a large state toward financial ruin and Al Gore would be making cheesy movies?

If you have not heard, Al Gore has made an alarmist movie about global warming called *An Inconvenient Truth*. It will probably be the biggest grossing PowerPoint presentation of all time and it will win an Oscar since the liberals will eat this up.

Just imagine the charisma of Al Gore and having to watch his science vacation slide show. But to comment fairly, I felt I needed to see this movie so that you do not have to. (I am nothing if not fair.) And for the record, when I see a liberally slanted movie like this I always pay for a different PG movie at the box office and sneak in, as I would never financially support such *Fahrenheit 9/11-type* propaganda.

Since Gore's movie is up against the blockbuster movie *The Da Vinci Code*, it will pale by financial comparison. One movie takes something we know well and twists the facts to spin a compelling story of intrigue. The other is about Jesus.

It seems clear to me that Al Gore believes we are heading toward a "planetary emergency" since he seems to be eating enough food to get him through a few years.

Global warming is probably a bunch of self-righteous, left-winged fashionable worries. I really have yet to be convinced that there is anything to global warming; and even if there is, I have always looked good in shorts and it might end the Winter Olympics, so that is a win-win for me.

The premise that Gore and his friends in the media are putting out is that there is "consensus" among scientists that global warming will have catastrophic consequences, and we humans caused it. Nothing could be further from proven truth.

Gore takes bits and pieces of tenured college professors' data (who will also apply for federal grants to solve the problem they have identified) and wants us to make a leap of faith that this great big world we live in is going to fall apart because you drive a Ford F150 truck instead of a moped to work. He quotes selected scientists in the piece, most of them with beards and still LSD-tripping from the '60s, and strings together plausible but not proven conclusions that we are causing this "planetary emergency."

These are the same environmentalists who fought nuclear power and forced us to build more coal plants that omit the CO_2 that is causing this. As we found out in the past, it is not in the nature of scientists and the media to over-hype something that makes us scared. Can you say Y2K?

We also know that they are trying to take a play out of the Clinton playbook. First, they say something like, "the debate in the scientific community is over." Then, on an unproven premise that gets echoed in the media, they proceed to act like they have the answer. You know, the same way Bush did on WMDs in Iraq. Wasteful funding is always best attained when those asking for the money do so breathlessly and say that it is an "emergency."

The reality is that there is no consensus in the scientific community over global warming. Richard S. Lindzen, who is the Alfred P. Sloan Professor of Meteorology, Department of Earth, Atmospheric and Planetary Sciences at MIT, wrote an opposing op-ed piece in the June 26 *Wall Street Journal*. He said this regarding global warming: "First, non-scientists generally do not want to bother with understanding the science. Claims of consensus relieve policy types, environmental advocates and politicians of any need to do so. Such claims also serve to intimidate the public and even scientists — especially those outside the area of climate dynamics. Secondly, given that the question of human attribution largely cannot be resolved, its use in promoting visions of disaster constitutes a bait and switch scam. That is an inauspicious beginning to what Mr. Gore claims is not a political issue but a 'moral' crusade."

Using the "moral" crusade card, Gore has presented his case to Congress, which, I would not suggest doing, since politicians seem to just be confused when something is moral. After making his case, Gore sat on the hood of his car in the congressional parking lot and told anyone who would listen that he used to go to school there.

Later that day he gave a passionate speech to a gathering about why George Bush broke the law and how Gore was going to fix global warming. Those who heard the speech described it as "the worst subway ride ever."

I am pretty sure Gore is just doing all of this for much-needed attention after losing an election he should have won. Liberals in the media have his back. He was even on the front of *GQ* magazine for his noble cause; apparently *GQ* gave George Clooney the month off.

It may shock you, but I happen to drive a hybrid car. It is a mix between a Hummer and a Lincoln Navigator. While I do not know if global warming is true or not, I am not going to alter my lifestyle in any major way based on these liberal types browbeating me with inconclusive science. The base years on which they are concluding that the Earth has warmed a fraction of a degree was 200 years ago. Remember, people back then did not have indoor plumbing and they were fighting off Indians; I am not sure I trust their thermometer readings enough to move to a commune in Vermont.

Maybe if it were not Al Gore pushing this story, I might take it more seriously. Al Gore could not win his home state of Tennessee when he ran for president; otherwise he would be our president and we would all be driving clown-like Shriner cars while he and his "limousine liberals" flew around in Air Force One. The more you know about him the less you like. About every other scene in his movie shows him on a private jet flying around and looking at Katrina-like damage with a maudlin air of concern.

The only proof I see that the Earth is warming is that Al Gore all of a sudden seems less frozen. Certainly an argument can be made to refreeze him.

By permission of Michael Ramirez and Creators Syndicate, Inc.

Capturing Saddam — A Brief ReCap

"If you define cowardice as running away at the first sign of danger, screaming and tripping and begging for mercy, then yes, Mr. Brave man, I guess I'm a coward."

— Jack Handey, Deep Thoughts on *Saturday Night Live*

Unless you've been living in a hole somewhere, you know that we caught Saddam Hussein last week. After exhorting his troops to fight to the death, U.S. solders found Hussein cowering in a hole in his underwear. Perfect!

Our brave troops, not heeding the sign on Saddam's door, "If this spider hole is rocking, don't come a knocking," apprehended this tin horn leader who had our government scared to death just a few years ago and ushered us into this wasteful war. Hell, Martha Stewart put up more of a fight when they arrested her.

I have developed three theories on Saddam's capture:

1. He was trying to disguise himself. Maybe — and this is just a theory at this stage — he was in the stark, unfurnished new home with $750,000 cash and some guns tying to disguise himself as a rap star. The fact that the MTV show *Cribs* was in preproduction to do an episode at his hole next week validates this thinking. The $750,000 was "soft money" intended for Bush's Democratic challenger.

In fact, I have suggested that there is so much corrupt money in politics that our elected officials should wear uniforms like NASCAR drivers with their sponsor's logo on them, identifying who has given them money to own them. It just seems fair, but I digress.

2. This was some kind of bad Groundhog Day. Saddam pops out of his hole and we get four more years of the Bush administration.

3. He thought cowering in a hole and hurling insults until the shooting ends worked for the French, so why not him? His next step was to ask for a big construction contract to rebuild Iraq. He could probably get it from our confused government.

U.S. troops pulled him out of this hole, and he said, "I am the president of Iraq and I am willing to negotiate." I am no West Point military tactician, but when you are in your tighty whities in a hole and fifty U.S. soldiers have their guns pointed at your head, I am not entirely sure what you have in the way of a "bargaining chip."

Sadly, Saddam had Spam, beans, hot dogs and soda in the hole, which is the closest the Bush administration has come to finding what he used to gas the Kurds.

A bounty of $25 million is supposed to be given to whoever turned him in. So if you see Mustafa in the nearby village, with his goat pimped out with gold chains and rims, you will know it was he. If no one claims the money, Bush will just instinctively give it to Halliburton.

The good news is that his time in the hole had not been a waste, as he learned to surrender in English. This clues you in that he knew what was coming. The soldier then said, "President Bush sends his regards."

Unless you're a Democratic presidential candidate, you have to love that! As it turns out, treating a brutal war tyrant with such sarcasm is in violation of U.N. Rule 6996 forbidding such, and the soldier will have to stand trial in The Hague for bravado in front of a prisoner.

So now that the U.S. has the leader of the Need-A-Bath Party, what do we do with him? Just to show the U.N. and the world that we are thorough, we had a bald medic examine his hair for weapons of mass destruction and then for effect, ran the tape eight million times in the next forty-eight hours on all U.S. 24-hour news stations. Then they took Saddam's DNA to make sure it was he. We should have been more sensitive to the fact that it might be embarrassing to the Iraqi people to see their president endure such treatment. We know all too well how embarrassing it is when your president is forced to submit to DNA sampling.

They then took him to an "undisclosed location," which I am sure startled a napping Dick Cheney when they traipsed in. They interrogated Saddam but decided not to de-brief him as he had new briefs still in the package back at the hole. I hope they water-boarded him, and, just to please the French, did so with Perrier.

Then we interrogate him. But sadly we can no longer beat information out of him based on U.N. rules. Not that he would give up information, but I think it would be fun to just beat him. Since we may not be able to technically "beat him" in traditional terms, we might want to bring in the French to help here. They could talk arrogantly and condescendingly about all they have done in military history and perhaps he will break down.

Better yet, maybe bring in Bobby Brown to slap him around a bit. Afterwards Saddam will say crazy stuff and perhaps break out in song for no apparent reason. But we know this with certainty: if we let Bobby get some community service hours by pounding him, he will always come back for more, perhaps even showing up at one of Bobby's court appearances in support.

Oddly enough, most Iraqis do not believe that Saddam is caught. From what I can gather from watching news footage of the Mideast, young male Iraqi men really need to be able to poke something with a stick and then dance around chanting in a guttural manner before it really sinks in. And not everyone wanted Saddam caught. His daughters, the as-yet-to-be-captured playing cards, mainstream media, and the nine Democratic presidential contenders chief are among them.

It was such a big event that, although it helped Bush, even the *New York Times* had to put it on the front page. Most liberal papers even stopped bashing Bush about the war for a few days to do so.

But make no mistake, they are hiding in the weeds. They did air Howard Dean's comment that "catching Saddam does not make the world a safer place." In all fairness, and considering all the foreign affairs experience Dean had as governor of Vermont, we really need to hear him out on this one.

Remember that just in the last month, Dean and the media sank to new lows by attacking Bush for not attending the funerals of the 350 soldiers killed in Iraq. I wonder if they checked to see if John F. Kennedy or Lyndon Johnson attended the 58,000 funerals created by the Vietnam War?

Now I predict we will try Saddam and execute him in short order. Unless, of course, he requests and gets his trial moved to California.

No Juan Left Behind

So weakened by his lack of popularity and public protest when he did attempt some reform, Bush did not adequately deal with illegal immigration. As a result, he punted to the Obama leftists the power to shape immigration policy.

Democrats came to power by dividing their supporters into classes based on perceived slights and victimization, placing immigrants in a special, fledgling growth area — a loyal voting bloc. Republicans, who view them as a cheap way to finish that rock wall in their backyard, never had the courage to address the issue. Democrats do not want self-reliant immigrants like Louisiana Governor Bobby Jindal for fear they might undermine their "All Minorities are Victims and Must be Subsidized to Succeed" platform. "Racist" Republicans do not want any Puerto Ricans for fear they might marry their daughters.

Even when we try to make English our official language, we meet with protest from Democrats and one Republican governor of California. Americans are tired of pressing 1 for English. It is my firm stance that all immigrants who come to our country should learn to speak our language; just like my ancestors did when they came here from England.

As poll after poll proves, we want English to be our way of communicating, followed closely by that Pig Latin-derived language Snoop Dogg uses in which every word ends with "snizzel."

If you do not think unfettered immigration can pose a problem for the existing inhabitants, just ask Native Americans (you may know them as Indians).

I have no problem with immigration; it is the illegal part that's troubling. Hard-working immigrants here legally in active pursuit of the American Dream delight me. But we should decide whom we let in; we should not just allow in the freeloaders (the future Democratic base) who think they are entitled to come here and lay claim to our largesse with an anchor baby. The Democrats say to illegals, "Come here and we will give you drivers licenses, welfare, health care — we are the Party of party favors to those who vote for us."

If a poor Guatemalan boy comes here and sells drugs or traffics in guns, which results in his arrest, we put him in a prison with a room, three meals a day and health care. That would put him on the Forbes 400 list of the wealthiest Guatemalans back home. So why not come here?

A writer for *Playboy* penned a detailed column on illegal immigration and why the immigrants come here. It was a "how to sneak into America" piece. The good news is that since it was in *Playboy*, no one actually read it.

Should immigration even be a federal issue, since illegals use mostly local services such as schools, hospitals, and police? It is estimated that an illegal family with kids in school costs a city $23,000 per year in services. With special English classes, some estimates are higher. Without a consumption-based "fair tax," illegals pay nothing toward their own keep. We pay their costs in property and sales taxes.

Gang activity is now mostly driven by illegal Hispanic immigrants. Thankfully, there are signs that Attorney General Eric Holder will be tough on at least some illegals. Last week he ceremoniously arrested 700 Mexican drug and gun dealers out west. He might have arrested them and charged them with capitalism, the worst crime anyone can commit in the eyes of the Obama administration.

Politicians find themselves in tall weeds here, wallowing in a problem of their own making. They look only to polls, not their consciences, for guidance on votes. My suggestion is simple: If someone wants to come to America, he or she must add value rather than be a drain.

I was reminded recently how our policies have changed when German scientist Konrad Dannenberg died in Alabama at age 96. He developed the rocket engine for the V-2 rocket for Nazi Germany. We brought him to the U.S., where he spearheaded our missile program that kept us safe. As his obituary should have said, he was survived by the human race. I feel strongly that persons like Dannenberg (and any Eastern European supermodel) should quickly be granted citizenship. We must replenish our reservoir of future Donald Trump wives.

We should decide who comes here. Taxpaying American citizens should not be put upon by those looking to take advantage of the government cheese plate the Democrats will offer. If an illegal wants to stay, he should have to serve in our military for his green card. Illegals have a long history of fighting in America. Ten thousand Mexicans fought at the Alamo; there would have been more, but they only had three cars.

Given the rising unemployment in the U.S., many of the illegals who came here for work are heading home. This leaves us with the ones who are here to mooch off of us or who are willing to live a life of crime; neither is positive for America. Unless a Dominican has a 97-mile-per-hour fast ball and pitches for the Braves, I feel he should not be here illegally.

Those immigrants who want to come here and are willing to do something of value for that privilege should be welcomed. Since they have long been willing to come here to do the work Americans are unwilling to do, I suggest their first job should be to write and enforce a coherent immigration policy for us.

Mourning the Passing of Common Sense

"The only thing that sustains one through life is the consciousness of the immense inferiority of everyone else. This is a feeling I have always cultivated."

— Oscar Wilde

I am always amazed as to what people do not know. There is a tendency for people to think that everyone else is smarter than they are. That is a big assumption, born of inferiority and TV's display of perfection that is usually not true. The successful people I know are the ones who can accept failure and forge ahead with resolve. You can measure a person by what it takes to discourage him or her. Dogged determination, confidence, vision, hard work, and common sense can win out over IQ and privilege almost all of the time. The most important of these is common sense — and I submit it is suffering a severe decline in the world today.

I am reminded of an old joke about three college graduates who were sentenced to execution in the electric chair. One is a University of Tennessee graduate, one a University of Florida grad and one an MIT grad. All three are brought on the same day to the execution chamber to be electrocuted for their crimes. The religious warden gives the University of Tennessee prisoner his last rites and tells the executioner to pull the lever. Sparks fly, there is a short, and the electric chair fails to work. The warden proclaims this to be an act of God and lets the UT grad go.

The second death row inmate is the Florida grad. He gets in the chair; the warden signals the executioner to pull the lever, and the same thing happens. Having seen the UT grad's stay of execution he gets up, the warden proclaims it an act of God, and the Florida prisoner quickly runs out of there.

Having seen all this, the MIT prisoner is next. He gets in the chair and the same thing happens: the warden calls for the lever to be pulled and the chair sparks and shorts out. The warden tells him he can leave, but the MIT grad cannot stop himself and says, "Hey wait, if you just connect that loose wire there with the fuse box ... ."

Common sense is rare, and it often comes down to what our parents taught us when we were young. Saying "Yes, sir" and "Yes, ma'am" goes a long way these days, as does looking folks in the eye. It has been said that 75 percent of success is having an alarm clock that works, so just showing up as promised puts you ahead of some sloths.

The other thing about common sense is that you should not let the media scare you into irrational actions. Take for example the swine/bird flu scare going around currently. Now, it is not like the media to take an isolated situation and trump it up into a nationwide scare, but they are doing it with the swine flu. Congress only showed concern until it realized the swine flu would not effect their pork barrel spending.

Apparently the bird flu scare this week has frightened many folks and many are not eating chicken now — which has nothing to do with getting the bird flu. People do irrational things. I admit that when the mad cow disease scare came around last year that, as a precaution, I stopped drinking Beefeater gin for a while. Once explained to me, I felt silly but soldiered on. Ironically, the Beefeater helped.

Common sense has died in this country. It has died a slow politically correct and bureaucratic death. I voted the GOP in to spend less, be more efficient, and reduce government. My disillusionment with them is at an all-time high. It was reported the other day that the government willingly spends 1.4 cents of our tax dollars to produce a penny. That is just the latest in a long line of wasteful things our government does.

Common sense has long eluded our government. Our response to the 9-11 attacks was to keep old ladies from carrying more that three ounces of shampoo on airplanes and forfeit more of our freedoms with wiretaps. For the last two years in the airports there has been a loud speaker announcement "Effective immediately from the Homeland Security office and TSA, no liquids or gels....." That announcement has been running for three years now. And should an attack alert happen, imagine all of the time it will take the TSA to look up in their federal manuals exactly what a code orange level is. "Hold up there Dewayne, stop frisking that eighty-three-year-old grandmother from Ohio, we need to find out if code orange is bad or good."

With wiretaps, TSA, spending, and new agencies in D.C., our government seems to insist on keeping us safe, whether we like it or not. No one seems to understand that this country, like Russia, will not be conquered by another country. The way we will create our own demise is by spending money now to avoid any pain in the moment, thereby ensuring that our kids will be encumbered with our selfish debt for generations. If this great experiment in democracy fails, it will be because of our reckless spending, not a foreign enemy.

Our country is in trouble for borrowing too much money, so the answer we get from Congress to fix things is to borrow more money. We have to remember that politicians are like alcoholics: they are always talking about how they are going to stop spending our money soon — right after their next binge.

Our politicians are no longer leaders, just one of those relatives always asking to borrow money. They are hucksters in drag, and their makeup is starting to run. We should no more let them spend our money than we should let Michael Jackson backstage at a Jonas Brothers concert.

My guess is that 90 percent of our problems today are because people are conditioned to value style over substance. It seems budding socialist Obama will be elected president, not on his ideas for America, since no one has even asked him about that, but because he is smooth. When Obama looks at them, reporters just swoon and nearly pass out. One reporter has asked Obama a tough question. All other news anchors are standing by to see when that guy gets fired for it.

The important job of asking tough questions and reporting died this year. Journalism as we know it no longer exists. So-called journalists are now cheerleaders for liberal ideas. That is why journalism is dying and newspapers will continue to struggle. I know because I read it in the paper online.

So let's say farewell to Common Sense and give it a proper obituary: "Common Sense was preceded in death by his parents, Truth and Trust; his wife, Discretion; his daughter, Responsibility; and his son, Reason. He is survived by two troublesome step-siblings, My Rights and Ima Whiner."

No Doubts About Death Penalty

The New York Times must have had to take a deep breath, but it did report that approximately twelve recent studies have determined that the death penalty saves lives and serves as a deterrent. It must be at least partially true if *The New York Times* published it.

Of course, instead of the headline "Death Penalty Saves Lives," *The Times* masked the clear results by titling the article "Does Death Penalty Save Lives? A New Debate." It is clear that all of the studies quoted showed that it does save lives, with some saying that for every execution, up to eighteen murders are prevented.

Once I was asked whether I was for or against the electric chair. The moderator knew my answer, but was shocked when I answered that I was against it. He asked why, and I said I opposed the use of the chair because we had waited too long. Rather, I was now in favor of electric bleachers, just until we could get caught up.

My father was in law enforcement and I have seen the worst of mankind, and it was not just at our family Thanksgiving dinners. A proud Hart family fact is that there have never been any murders at our family dinners. This is amazing, since the mixture of tense pent-up animosity, booze, and the readily accessible turkey carving knife would put the odds very high for a least one murder.

It is very clear to me both on intuitive and practical levels that certain and swift consequences for killing (and in my view, molesting or raping) another person should be imposed by our society. In short, we simply should say, "If you kill someone, we will kill you back." I am sure the actual statute would contain more legal verbiage than that, but the message should be the same.

Now there is always the liberal, knee-jerk reaction that we, in the course of frying 1,000 of our lowest forms of life, might convict an innocent man. But in my view, that is the cost of doing business. I would say to these folks that with advances in DNA evidence, surveillance cameras, and other law enforcement technologies, there would be fewer mistakes in the future.

In reading Norman Mailer's obit recently, I was reminded that this liberal icon was the toast of New York City and the media when he won the release of a convicted murderer. But there was just a small footnote: The guy murdered again within weeks of his release. Oops! Remember, liberals want a moratorium on the death penalty just for the murderer, not his victims.

I encourage you to read about the "BTK killer" (Bind, Torture and Kill), who murdered ten people from 1974 until 1991. He was the second leading cause of death in Kansas during that time frame; the first was boredom. If you dig past the 2005 arrest headlines that he was his church congregation president, you will discover a fact that is very telling: By his own admission, he stopped in 1991 when Kansas adopted the death penalty.

If you have ever sat on a trial, you know that almost all the benefit of the doubt goes to the defendant. We, through our tax dollars, provide an inordinate amount of legal support to capital murder defendants. In Atlanta, millions of dollars have been spent on the defense of Brian Nichols, even though his murders of four people were caught on camera as he shot his way out of a courthouse in 2005. Believe me, if someone goes to trial for murder, there is overwhelming evidence because states cannot afford too many of these trials.

For us to be ashamed in the world's eyes for employing the death penalty is misplaced. We have as evolved a legal system as any country in the world. For that, we should make no apologies. Many Middle Eastern countries barbarically cut off hands for stealing, and cut off operative body parts for adultery. Bill Clinton does not travel to these countries.

Liberal politicians publically lament us using "enhanced interrogation techniques" on terrorists. I guess they prefer that we ask nicely for information. In the game that is Washington political wordplay, they like to call what we do "torture."

I have full confidence in juries across the country to do the right thing when it comes to voting for a murder conviction (except in Los Angeles). Every jury I have sat on has given me a good feeling about the people in the community. It even looks like high roller O.J. Simpson is going to finally get his due when Las Vegas comps his room and food for the next five to eight, depending on when he gets paroled. Note to kids out there, you might be able to double murder your wife and her friend, but never steal a man's bobblehead doll sports memorabilia collection.

The profiles of capital cases are so high, and there are so many anti-death penalty groups out there that will pounce on egregious prosecutions, I feel justice is served. Yet, even if convicted, murderers sit on death row for appeal after appeal until they die of old age. Scott Peterson, who killed his pregnant wife, might be young enough to live through years of appeals and actually be executed on death row. I would love to pull the lever on that one, and would gladly go out to California with my buddies and a cooler of beer to make a weekend of it.

It comes down to the simple view that the most violent people only understand the fear of such violence on themselves. Reasoning with them and "trying to understand them" just do not work. And clearly, we have to be careful about executing minors. It is something that we rarely do, but when done, it certainly makes teenagers think twice about carrying a fake I.D.

Bailouts for Bankrupts
Bad for Business

In the second most regulated business behind banks, insurance giant AIG (the same company that snookered our federal government out of $170 billion to pay its obligations) is in the news again.

Congress, having no idea how a good business works, did what it does best. It mindlessly threw our tax money at yet another company uttering breathless warnings of calamity. I would remind the Obama administration that "hope" is not a business plan or strategy for governing.

For our $170 billion, Congress bought us 80 percent ownership of, and thus responsibility for, AIG. Responsibility is another thing Congress does not do well. Much like its stewardship of Freddie Mac, Fannie Mae, Amtrak, the Postal "Service," etc., Congress fumbled this one.

Let's face it folks, government could not run a church bake sale. Yet inexplicably, many of us want to turn more of our economy, health care, and private lives over to politicians. With Cap and Trade, the sky is literally not the limit to what they want to tax and control.

The stimulus bill, written by Democrats, passed by Congress, and signed by President Obama, included a provision for AIG to pay contractually obligated bonuses of less than .01 percent of their bailout money.

After the public reacted to AIG's bonus plan, the thespians in Congress feigned outrage. If there is anything politicians do well, it is acting angry about something they did — followed closely by pointing fingers and sidestepping issues. Shucking, jiving, and whoring round out the top five.

Elected officials are that rare breed of multi-taskers who can both cause a problem and be incensed by the results. As long as 51 percent of us are dumb enough to buy it, they stay in their gerrymandered and lobbyist-dominated offices.

Claims by AIG executives that they deserve the bonuses are credible, since they were smart enough to effectively steal $170 billion taxpayer dollars in the first place.

It is rich that Congress, which ran up an $11 trillion deficit, bankrupted the country, and then raised its own pay, tells others how to run their financial affairs.

This is particularly ironic as it relates to jets (which, behind other people's pay, is the only thing Congress seems to fixate on) in light of Nancy Pelosi's demand for a larger personal jet to chauffeur her back and forth to California — presumably so she can preach to us about using too much fuel.

Senator Chris Dodd, D-Conn., who lied about his role until caught dead to rights — which is the only time a politician comes clean — inserted the language allowing AIG, coincidentally based in his home state, to pay these bonuses.

And oh by the way, Dodd and Obama were the top two recipients of donations from AIG last year, followed by Fannie Mae and Freddie Mac when they sought a bailout.

See any trends developing?

With all the blood on their hands, both Obama and Dodd were able to conjure up outrage. It is akin to O.J.'s outrage at the murder of his ex-wife; like O.J., they have vowed to get the culprits.

In retrospect, if George Bush had wanted to protect the U.S., he would have invaded the credit default swap department at AIG or the Senate Banking Committee instead of Iraq.

In the same way we only learn geography when we invade a country, Americans only learned about credit default swaps when forced to pick up the tab for someone else's poorly calculated risks. Each administration teaches us something. Bill Clinton's presidency taught a nation about DNA testing on dresses.

Credit default swaps are nothing but off-track betting, where one company promises to back bond payments from another. This is like Mafia protection money, only with less transparency. Allowing the gamblers to default would have been fine for our country. I made this case early on in this bailout mania; just let the free markets sort out the winners and losers like it has for generations. Why subsidize the bad companies?

When the government props up clearly insolvent companies, we have a fake economy. Distrust of this manipulated market makes the usual economic metrics unreliable and creates a dangerous business landscape.

Private business owners, who risk their capital and make sensible decisions, are forced to compete with inefficiently run, yet politically connected companies.

The most disturbing event coming out of the AIG mess is the ability of politicians to single out someone who has been paid in accordance with a legal contract and to tax him 90 percent. This political retribution where Congress governs out of anger should scare us all.

The great thing about leaving business owners alone is that if they make stupid mistakes, they lose money and go bankrupt. Smarter operators move in and the consumer wins. It is the purest and best way to weed out bad companies. Let the free market work since, as we all know, government does not.

It is amazing how well capitalism works in the absence of meddling politicians.

By permission of Michael Ramirez and Creators Syndicate, Inc.   www.IBDeditorials.com/cartoons

Washington Stars in 'Bailouts Gone Wild'

In my ongoing quest to unburden you from worthwhile reading, I felt it my duty to opine on the recent heartfelt requests by smut merchants Larry Flynt and Joe "Girls Gone Wild" Francis for a federal bailout. This brings a whole new meaning to stimulus package.

Those who were lucky enough to get up to their eyeballs in debt back in 2007 when it was as easy as signing your name, are getting bailed out. Why not let everyone get into the game? Hey, it's free money, ain't it? So we get the moans by porn entrepreneurs Flynt and Francis, both in their movies, and now for some of that sweet bailout money that Congress is tossing around.

Clearly Bush is to blame for the problems in the porn industry. Bill Clinton would have never let it get so bad.

Perhaps their requests should be taken as seriously as others since the porn industry employs more than 10,000 in the Los Angeles area alone. Many of the male actors may have to go back to actually delivering pizzas for real. Recent hardships in the industry have resulted in half of the workers losing their jobs. That means 4,000 "actors," 2,000 "actresses," 800 cameramen, 400 fluffers and one writer. I think his name is Murray.

And when any industry is in trouble, the ripple effect through the economy can take its toll. My not-distant-enough uncle has seen his business revenues drop. He owns a small yet prestigious porn acting school in Tennessee. Tuition is often funded by those student loan companies that you see advertising on mass transit.

Most classes somehow revolve around a doorbell being rung, either

by a pizza deliveryman or a plumber. Many of his students have gone on to win acting honors in the annual adult movie actors' guild awards. While Hollywood calls its award an Oscar, I think they call theirs a Woody.

If the feds do come to the rescue of the smut industry, they will want to appoint a porn czar as they are prone to do, because the drug czar and the like have worked so well. I think they just like naming someone a czar — it makes them feel all-powerful. Congress is like the Shriners, sans the funny hats but with an unlimited club budget.

Since we are heading down the path of Russia, why not name our leaders who manage subsets of the economy czars? It just is starting to make sense. Slick Willie is looking to get back into the game, so I suggest we name him porn czar.

Being a free-market capitalist, I would prefer that the private sector step up and help out these women in need. No so much the men. I will, along with some of my better guy friends, propose a foundation that would reach out to these unemployed women and offer them housing and comfort.

Perhaps I will call it Habitat for Hookers. I can just feel the Nobel Prize committee taking notice of my efforts. Along the lines of a private market solution to this problem, I would suggest retraining some of these workers, perhaps in the area of tax preparation, since they seem to like to work with people and in situations where someone gets screwed.

But be real specific when you ask one of them to handle your extension — that could get awkward.

Retraining the men may be tougher; perhaps they could become gas station attendants. If we could keep them from pulling the gas hose out and spraying the car when they are done, it might just work.

This latest request punctuates the absurdity of what we have become. We are moonwalking up the slippery slope of financial disaster set by Congress with its own special blend of social engineering, government intervention, spending for the moment, and utter incompetence. It has privatized profits and socialized losses with its meddling in corporate America, all the while putting itself at the center of it all.

With the bailouts, we are putting at risk what made this country great — free-market capitalism.

The Gay Marriage Thing Ain't Going Away

California, that liberal, big spending, high-tax state that is going broke, found time last week to intrude in yet another area mucked up by its high-minded attempts at control: gay marriage. Proposition 8, which bans same-sex marriage, was narrowly passed by California voters.

Even metro-sexual liberal Republican Governator Arnold Schwarzenegger came out against gay marriage. I found that highly curious from a man who spent the majority of his formative years being oiled up by other men and posing with them in a Speedo.

I predicted this in a column last year that began with: The courts in California, which are more like the courts of Caligula, recently ruled that gays can marry, thus launching the state's first wave of gay marriages that did not involve Liza Minnelli. While this is great news for California's leather chaps business, it is a big slap in the face for the voters who will probably overturn this ruling.

The vote was made possible when Republican constitutional lawyers filed suit against the State of California for allowing 18,000 gay marriages under the court ruling last year. It may be their last chance to make money since, between the Bush wiretaps and the Obama "empathy-driven" interpretation of the law, the Constitution may not be around much longer to defend.

If it were up to some hard right Republicans, gays not only could not get married, they could not even be wedding planners.

I have long said that I do not care what consenting gay dudes do as long as they do not do it to me. Unless I fall asleep in the stall of a

Greyhound bus station bathroom or on Senator Larry Craig's couch, I should be fine. And I fully understand those in the majority who are against gay marriage. Yet the cool thing about my side of the debate is that those who do not want gay marriage do not have to get gay married. It is their choice, which is the best thing about freedom.

While I am not a fan of the mechanics of gay male relationships, as someone who values freedoms and personal responsibilities, I do not believe it is the government's role to regulate what two consenting people do. From my research on the gay issue, I have come to realize that I would not be a lesbian. It just seems like a lot of work and requires an attention to detail that I lack.

Why should gays be denied the pleasures of "till death do we part," losing half their stuff, and paying alimony to someone they have grown to hate?

Guess who said this: "America is a free society, which limits the role of government in the lives of our citizens. In this country, people are free to choose how they live their lives." It was George W. Bush, the same guy who tried to put an anti-gay marriage bill before Congress. I suspect he did that at the behest of Dick Cheney, who was trying to get out of paying for his lesbian daughter's wedding.

It seems that the "sanctity of marriage" is only threatened in an election year or when the GOP is behind in the polls. That hypocrisy, and unconscionable spending, are why many of us left the Republican Party.

It harkens back to the "Old" in the Grand Old Party, where the Strom Thurman-brand of politics ("Lookie there fellers, there they are, let's get 'em") plays to the worst in us, just as the Democrats' politics of envy plays to the worst in our human nature.

I respect Miss California's statement of her belief against gay marriage. It is truly her view, and the liberal media devoured her for it. Yet her view is the same one that Barack Obama professed. Isn't it interesting how the media conveniently ignores that? Could it be that Miss California gave her honest feelings on the matter and Obama is masking his views in the name of political expediency? As soon as his teleprompter tells him to change his stand, Obama will.

The subject of same-sex marriage is difficult for most people, and I respect Miss California more than I do Barack Obama for stating her true feelings on the matter. But, when faced with a tough choice, I find erring on the side of personal liberty and freedom is the right thing to do. I think our Founding Fathers would agree. Remember, they wrote the Constitution in powdered wigs and tight silk pants with ornate buttons. Most paintings depict them with their hands on their hips, looking very dramatic. I think they would side with the gays.

God, Guns, and Gays

Three particular issues arouse passions like no other. These litmus test subjects (and I feel very confident asserting this) are God, Guns, and Gays. Given the emails that I get when I write on any of these topics, they evoke more unreasoned emotion than anything else.

God, Guns, and Gays, which I also think was my high school prom theme, can cause family rifts, chasms in relationships, and outright irrational behavior in humans.

Other writers have suggested that if I want to be liked I shouldn't go near God, Guns, or Gays. But my thinking is that I have never been liked, so why start trying so late in the game? Moreover, there are 300 million people in the U.S. (180 million of them here legally) and it is a fool's game to try to please them all, so here goes.

First about God: When this subject comes up, people are usually referring to their own particular deity, and therein lies the problem. Almost any action can be justified by someone's religion, most of which are based on books written more than 1,000 years ago, and open to all sorts of interpretations.

We must remember, moreover, that only 30 percent of the world's population is Christian and that those 2.1 billion Christians belong to upwards of 150 different denominations that slice and dice the Bible in their own way, even within a denomination. We are in a war now because a certain sect takes a jihadist view of The Koran. All of this, if you read history, never ends well.

The Pilgrims came to the United States to flee religious persecution and to worship as they chose. With that in mind, our Founding Fathers made the separation of church and state one of the fundamental tenets of our democracy. They were clear; they wanted a democracy, not a theocracy. They wanted both freedom of, and freedom from religion.

So, when it emerges that upwards of 150 young graduates of the late Jerry Falwell's Liberty University are holding down important jobs in the Bush Administration, it starts to concern me.

And when one of the most senior staffers in the office of Attorney General Alberto Gonzalez, who recently resigned under pressure and took the Fifth Amendment, turns out to be a graduate of Falwell's fourth-tier law school, it is clear that mixing religion and law seems to be the objective.

Why must conservatives use lawyers who seek to codify their religious views and liberals install Ivy League-educated idealistic idiots who want to redress every slight and ill of mankind in the past, both real and imagined? Why not just a few state university-educated lawyers who just want to enforce the law fairly?

Many of these zealots do not recognize the separation of church and state, much in the same way that they do not recognize fellow parishioners in the liquor store.

Now on to guns: In the wake of the Virginia Tech tragedy, guns have become topical again. And again, like all matters of importance, less government intrusion in the matter is best. Liberals like Rosie O'Donnell spend much of their airtime on shows like *The View* preaching more gun control laws. And if you think guns make people criminals, then spoons are what made Rosie fat; therefore we should really outlaw spoons. And if government regulates our spoons, could forks and knifes be far behind?

Remember, three of the Fort Dix terrorist suspects had been in our country illegally for about twenty years. Between them, they had seventy-five arrests and citations over that time, and our crack government agents failed to investigate their illegal status.

Put no faith in government's ability to effectively police anything; you will be eternally disappointed. Government cannot police itself, much less others. Politicians in Washington could not run a high school musical, and certainly should not endeavor to nationalize health care. Bureaucrats go to work each day and only think about one thing — where to go for lunch.

Lastly, gays: Homosexuality, as we all know from televangelists, is a learned behavior. Much like those with cerebral palsy and red hair, folks who are gay "chose" it. Right?

All a gay guy has to do is close his mind to Brad Pitt and pray a lot and he will be fine. Not as fine as Brad Pitt, but okay. And what better way to make amends for the way you are than to spend your life in constant denial of the way you are so that you can please the pious people who hate you in the name of their religion?

If the real reason that those who condemn gay marriage do so because they do not want gays having sex, my suggestion is quite the opposite. As most married folks have found, there is no better way reduce the incidence of sex than to get married. The Religious Right may want to rethink that one.

Mixing various religious interpretations and civil law is a slippery slope. Mormons, who have one of the more interesting interpretations of religion, have funded anti-gay marriage campaigns. They feel strongly that marriage should be held sacred between a man and as many young wives that he can afford — ditto for the Muslims.

Some gays want to serve in the military. Perhaps drawn in by the lure of training at Fort Dix, gay men who want to risk their lives in Iraq and Afghanistan should be allowed to. And why harass them? If they risk their lives for our country, we ought to allow them Oscar Parties on base once a year.

Perhaps there is a role for them in the war, even if it is not in combat. I would suggest counterintelligence because, even though they do not like messy combat (except for gladiator movies), they can be vicious gossips. Maybe they could seduce closeted commanders of enemy units. Talk about your counterinsurgency!

Lesbian marriages, in the gayest of gay states Vermont, has been nothing but symbolic. Even the first lesbian couple who were wed in that "in your face Christian Right" service has already filed for divorce; I think they sited irreconcilable similarities.

As a favorite pastime, I enjoy reading the wedding announcements of gay couples in *The New York Times* and trying to discover which set of parents they are trying to piss off the most. Try it; it can be more fun than the crossword puzzle.

In conclusion, Bush and the neo-cons seem to want us to fight for our God, with guns, and without gays, to preserve the American way of life as they see it against Muslim terrorists. Given his popularity numbers, we are with him in this semi-religious war.

Life is really short, so spending too much time pushing our views about these personal matters on others is a waste of time. Live a good life, be an example for others, and then you will find that is the best way of encouraging people to see things your way.

A Little Pyongyang
for Bill Clinton

I thought things were going to get boring after Obama appropriated and Congress voted itself $550 million for a few new big private jets. Then our elected representatives got out of D.C., leaving only the hookers and DUI attorneys behind to suffer.

But who saves the day for us political humorists? Why, "Rambo" himself, Bill Clinton.

Slick Willie was in the U.S. recently because there was no need for him to travel. Hillary was in Africa. I know she was there because I saw her on TV dancing with various African tribes, thus giving the dictator-run, impoverished continent what it needs most: her gift of dance.

While the wife's away, Bill gets a call asking him to go to North Korea. He says he is real busy with Hillary gone and all, but thanks for the offer. Then the caller says there are two young Asian-American women who need help, so he yells to his personal assistant, "Clear my schedule!" Who would be more adept at sneaking women out of compromising situations than Bill Clinton?

All Democratic ex-Presidents and even ex-Vice Presidents should expect to get at least one Nobel Peace Prize and maybe an Oscar. It is as predictable as a porn star getting an STD. But would Bill Clinton become the Pete Rose of the liberal prize-giving establishment and be shunned? Had they not taken notice of his work on AIDS or the bluegrass duet he did with Paula Jones? Perhaps a grand gesture would be needed. And if he could upstage Barack Obama and please his wife, a charter member of the Ya Ya Sisterhood of the Traveling Pantsuit, even better.

Bill Clinton did what he normally does: he borrowed a jet from one of his Hollywood buddies and took it to pick up younger women. All he had to do was give credibility to, and kiss the tiny booty of, four-foot-tall, mini-dictator Kim Jong Il, to whom his wife and we as a nation are currently not speaking.

Lil' Kim required Bill Clinton to have a picture taken with him, which did nothing to dispel Asian stereotypes. Kim, of course, wore the crazy dictator haute couture of choice these days, the zip-up beige jacket. Nothing says "bat mess crazy" like despotic leaders such as Ahmadinejad or Kim Jong Il rocking one of those Members Only jackets. Nothing says "I am due respect" more than a windbreaker.

Al Gore, for whom these young women worked, was rejected as the emissary. A military C-5 transport plane was not available to fly his CO2-emitting girth to North Korea anyway. Yet he did fly (presumably with a nice, self-aggrandizing, carbon footprint) to California so he could be there for the photo-op when the plane returned.

Clearly, the parents of the two young women were torn on the event. On one hand, their daughters were freed from a hard labor prison camp in a cold, harsh, third-world, Communist country. On the other, the young women had to fly for thirteen hours in a private jet with Bill Clinton. Most would call this quandary the yin and yang of dilemmas.

It is unknown how much Obama had to do with this. Presumably, like shooting those Somali pirates, he would wait to see how it turned out before taking credit for it or condemning it. My guess is that he had to be in favor of the mission for Clinton to get the OK to go there. I cannot go to Cuba to get cigars, so I guess Obama had to have the imprimatur of the State Department. I wonder if Bill knew someone there.

I like what Clinton did, as it shows how quickly the private sector can respond to a crisis. He got a movie producer friend's jet, spent only $200,000 of non-taxpayer money, and acted swiftly and with resolve. Imagine the cost, time, and all the UN resolutions it would take for our government to help two people held captive. So, for the U.S. the score stands: two saved from Communism.

There is no word yet on the other 23 million people left starving in North Korea or when, if we stay on the trajectory Obama has planned for us, our country will be in the same situation.

Celebrity

© Copyright 2009 John Cole – All Rights Reserved.

Good-bye to Neverland

I do not know if you have heard yet because the media is really playing it down, but entertainment icon Michael Jackson died recently. Each news outlet has its own angle on this event, mostly involving 24-hour mindless speculation. So I thought: Who better to pontificate wildly on this subject without knowing what the heck he is talking about than yours truly?

Besides the public memorial at L.A.'s Staples Center, there is also to be a service at the Neverland Ranch crime scene. The evidence tags have been removed, and this future Dis-Graceland is now available to the media. Neighbors are torn on this possibility because Neverland has always been an enigma to them. For years they thought it was a middle school for boys.

Michael Jackson might be buried as all his heirs would like, and as his father-in-law, Elvis Presley, was (and as I want to be some day), near his own gift shop. Nothing dignifies a man's life like people being able to pay their respects and buy a shot glass with his picture on it to commemorate the somber moment.

Like most iconic and out-of-control stars, Jackson will be worth more dead than when he was alive and spending like a Congressman. This will be a financial blow to the Jackson family. If stage father Joe Jackson knew that the Lord was going to take one of his sons, he would have offered Tito first.

Because he morphed before our eyes from a black male into a white woman, I did not realize that many consider Michael Jackson a person who broke racial barriers. Maybe they mean that he started off black and worked his way toward becoming white. He clearly was a talented guy with deep-seated personal issues, but Rosa Parks he was not. Even rival attention junkies Jesse Jackson and Al Sharpton could not sell that one to the American people. Perhaps their last chance at selling that particular myth died with Billy Mays.

When you think of Michael Jackson, you have to also think of the children — and how best to keep them away from Michael Jackson. He violated the "three tykes and you're out" rule long ago.

Apparently he had a tortured childhood, just like most people who are in therapy after making hundreds of millions of dollars. The main thing I want to know is who fathered his kids. It was obvious that Michael was not interested in the mechanics of baby making, but he clearly liked kids — truly a dilemma.

From what I read, Michael married his dermatologist's assistant, Debbie Rowe, so she would bear him some kids. It has been reported that his dermatologist, Dr. Arnie Klein, was the sperm donor father of the two oldest Jackson kids, Prince One and Paris. Perhaps Michael did open the world's eyes to the racial possibilities of an African-American entertainment legend marrying a redneck's daughter (Lisa Marie Presley) and then having Jewish kids. Since there is no Jewish mother in the mix, I wonder how the kids will be raised. If child celebrity history is any guide, they will be raised by the media and the court system.

Many are taking Jackson's death hard, which surprises me. I never take any celebrity that seriously, but some do. A friend from Memphis told me that he called down to Raiford's Bar to ask if there was anything going on in connection with Michael's death. The club owner said she was "tore up about it," and my friend told her to hang in there. She said, "Baby we are. All we can do is take it one drink at a time."

The cautionary tale that was the life of Michael Jackson is one that we learn over and over. Never surround yourself with "yes men" who will only feed your demons instead of telling you "no" when they know they should. We have lost a talented performer who lived a tragic life. I hope his death will teach us to avoid drug addiction, false friends, and living for too long in Neverland.

Trump's Card: Pageants Full of Girls Going Wild

"A woman should dress to attract attention.
To attract the most attention, a woman should
be either nude or wearing something as expensive
as getting her nude is going to be."

— P.J. O'Rourke

For some un-encouraged reason, both of my daughters like to be in beauty pagents. I guess it beats my son wanting to be in one, but still it is a test for an ADD heterosexual father to sit through these things. My friends say I am so hyper-ADD that I would double park at a bordello. They seem to know a lot about bordello parking I reply, but they have a point.

Like most situations I have to endure but dislike, I simply throw money at it and run. And before you get all Dr. Phil on me about not being there for my daughters and missing that part of their lives, I have five words for you: video cam and Photoshopped pictures.

Despite my misgivings, my girls have learned a good bit from these pageants in the area of being a proper American woman: poise, confidence, and spending money. Boys have confidence, usually for no reason at all; and young girls, who should be confident, are not. Pageants, I reasoned, help correct this imbalance.

The contests my teenagers enter are more about their GPAs and less about T & A. So you might imagine how upset I was when Donald Trump got into the business of the T & A part with his Miss Universe Pageant.

I was deeply saddened this year by the news that Miss Kentucky, Tara Conner, almost had to relinquish her Mikimoto tiara after winning the Trump Miss USA title. This followed reports that she had tested positive for cocaine and, according to two delighted male witnesses, was seen making out with Miss Teen USA in a bar. So much for goals of "world peace" or helping crippled children.

Then two days later, Miss Nevada USA, Katie Rees, was stripped of her title by doing something heretofore thought impossible — bringing shame to the state of Nevada.

Fortunately, a higher power intervened to forgive Tara of her sins and restore dignity to the crown. Who, you might ask, would have the pious standing, dignity, and moral imperative to grant such forgiveness? Why, none other than the humble one with a golden cat tiara on his head too, "The Donald."

Laugh if you will (and I hope you do, as I write satire), but Donald Trump is a man full of second chances. His marriages and his hairstylist come to mind.

Trump surmised that since Conner was from a small town in the South (i.e., to his way of thinking, dumb) that the lure of the Big Apple made her weak. Donald knows this as Marla Maples was plucked by him the second she arrived from Dalton, Georgia. Marla was a beauty queen herself from the Carpet Capital of the World. I believe she even won the Miss Rug Burn crown once.

Now I know that Tara's home state of Kentucky is not as sophisticated as New York, even if the state flower is a satellite dish. Even though her crown for winning Miss Kentucky was made of duct tape, making fun of the South is getting old. Never mind that George Clooney also hails from there, and since the women are so ugly and ornery in the Northeast, they have developed a fondness for Southern beauty queens. Even if they were to find a good-looking Miss New Jersey, it is hard to win when your talent is hotwiring a car while smoking a cigarette.

While these women almost lost their chance to be Miss Kentucky or Miss Nevada, they greatly enhanced their chance to become the next Mrs. Charlie Sheen. Since mindless and lewd behavior has become the new rocket ship to celebrity, these girls know they do not need talent and patience to achieve their 15 minutes of fame. Pioneering role models like Pamela Anderson, Paris Hilton, Nicole Ritchie, Lindsay Lohan, Britney Spears, and Courtney Love have broken the skank glass ceiling for these girls.

These cheesy pageants do not even pretend to measure a contestant's

IQ and devotion to good causes, as do scholarship pageants like Miss America. Trump's pageants are tawdry displays of young women for publicity. They probably ought to just go ahead and put a brass pole on the stage of these contests and let the judges vote with crumpled $1 bills, since that is the next logical step for many of these women.

At first I was going to jump on The Donald for this decision, but when Rosie O'Donnell did just that, I realized that I could not possibly be on the same side of an issue as her and quickly took Trump's side. It is Donald's pageant and he can do with it what he will, I reasoned. Yet, I wonder what message it sends to Donald's next wife, who is probably still riding her tricycle, playing with dolls, and living somewhere in a former Soviet Union break-off Republic.

Trump, always the businessman, saw the potential of exploitation of women, not only by marrying them, but by displaying them to the world in the form of a pageant. He studied the pageant business and determined that they all had one thing missing: he was not getting a cut. So he bought The Miss USA and Miss Universe pageants on the cheap 10 years ago.

While the more traditional pageants that my daughters have won, like Miss Teen Georgia, boast of past winners like Phyllis George, Diane Sawyer, Deborah Norville, Halle Berry, Sophia Loren, Paula Zahn, Raquel Welch, Marla Maples, and a Donald Trump wife to be named later, are more wholesome events, The Donald getting into this business in the age of tawdry tabloid TV will only serve to demean it. Even Oprah Winfrey, the future spiritual leader of the world, won a Miss Black Tennessee pageant. And who is better than Trump to wet his beak in such flesh peddling? As lawyer Robert Steed says, he already looks like a look-out for a massage parlor.

While all the focus has been on his Miss USA pageant, I think his other pageant, Miss Universe, needs scrutiny too. Having watched it for years now, I have long felt that the Miss Universe pageant must be rigged as someone from Earth wins every year.

Jensen Hart and Hollis Hart being crowned as pageant winners.

Goin' Country

"I hate every bone in her body, but mine."

— Country music song by Tom Mabe

It was a big night for the Hart family recently when my daughter, who attends Vanderbilt in Nashville, got us third-row seats at the Country Music Awards there.

The reason that I like the CMAs so much is that it is the only awards show that did not give an obligatory award to Al Gore and it is made up of real people who sing real songs about life that we can relate to. Contrast that to other forms of music, which seems only to focus on "da bitches and hos."

That's the difference between holding an event in Nashville as opposed to the boring Oscar and Emmy events in Hollywood each year. (Then there is the Golden Globes, given by the foreign press. And if there were something that I dislike more than Hollywood, it would be the foreign press.)

The CMA puts on an entertaining show that does not include boring liberal political speeches or stupid categories like "Best Sound in a Short Story" or "Foreign Global Warming Documentary."

With Al Gore winning the liberal trifecta of an Emmy, Oscar, and a Nobel Peace Prize, he has to be happy. But I bet what he really wants is a CMA for Best Bluegrass Duet.

To look at Al these days, the real "inconvenient truth" he needs to come to terms with is that each Big Mac has 1500 calories. If he gets any fatter, he could personally cool Nashville by providing shade for the whole city. Al, you may be a big movie producer now with your Chicken Little "Sky Is Falling" slide show winning Hollywood awards, but the whole Orson Welles look is not working for you.

The producers of these Hollywood award shows seem to have forgotten that they are in the entertainment business. If actors want to run for political office, that is a different forum. The CMAs seem to have it figured out.

The CMA was a nice Tennessee event, one that Fred Thompson would historically attend. Sadly, Thompson's campaign manager had to step down that day for past gambling, drinking, cheating, and womanizing allegations, so he could not attend.

On the bright side, he will write a country song about it and be up for Best New Country artist next year. Worry not for Fred Thompson — if he does not win the presidency he can always go back to his job as a fake District Attorney and investigate the winner.

Country tends to have relatively stable and down-to-earth stars, in contrast to the pop music category that has brought us the likes of Michael Jackson and Britney Spears, who are train wrecks.

Unlike Britney, who seeks to balance motherhood with her "comeback" from her last comeback, country stars do not seem to create the publicity drama that she does when she is drunk and showing her lady business all over town. My worst nightmare (and her kids') is her comeback does not work and she will be forced to be a full-time mom.

And there was no self-promoting huckster like Donald Trump on the CMAs. Instead the host was James Denton, a Nashville native, University of Tennessee alum and resident hottie plumber on *Desperate Housewives*. Trump, on the other hand, would have had to call his show *Desperate Hair Weaves*.

I go through my country music phase about every six years or so and I am back in the early stages of one again. And my how it has changed!

The good news is how country music has been expanded in recent years. Jamie Foxx, Kid Rock, and Darius Rucker of Hootie and the Blowfish fame were all part of country music's biggest night. Who would have thought that!

One bit of inside info on the CMAs came from my daughter. She said the audience booed the Dixie Chicks. Yet, when I watched it on Tivo, it was clearly dubbed over with applause by ABC — so much for media fairness.

I found that interesting, and it was clearly anticipated by ABC, as the show was live. I do respect the Chicks speaking their mind, but they have to respect their peers' response. It is not smart to bite that hand that feeds you.

Anyway, enough as an entertainment correspondent. I just like the way that country music has always represented real people in America, their struggles, joys, cowboy hats, and blue jeans. The patriotism and Southern values that country music has always shown make me proud of this country and the performers of this music.

Arrested Developments: Celebrities and Their Award Shows

"Acting is a child's prerogative. Children are born to act. Usually, people grow up and out of it. Actors always seem to me to be people who never quite did grow out of it."

— Joanne Woodward

In the annual ritual of self-adulation of Hollywood by Hollywood and for Hollywood, the Oscars award season began this week. It is the time of the year that our national celebrities take time to give themselves much-needed attention. Traditionally, this season lasts from January until November, leaving December open for celebrities to spend a week in rehab before being arrested at Christmas.

For me, this year's Oscars were as special as the others. In all humility, it was an honor for me to not be nominated again for, as we refer to any award show in my house, "Passover."

It saddens me that many of our biggest stars are regularly incarcerated. They seem to drop like flies once they achieve a certain amount of notoriety and fame, so much so that we have to have shows like *American Idol* and *America's Next Drunken Star* to replenish the supply of luminaries that we lose to our criminal justice system each week. Troubled celebrities in Tinseltown are as expected as lying about your age and botched plastic surgery is in that city.

The trouble for our stars often begins with their dance with the paparazzi, which they seem to invite early in their careers. At some point, they begin to find it irritating to be constantly chased around while clubbing, wearing no underwear, sunbathing topless, and getting caught on tape in the process of hitting or cursing the photographer.

It is the main reason I am done with porn. Don't get me wrong, the money was good, but the lifestyle takes its toll. This narcissistic flirtation with the cameras ends up leading to the demise of these flash-in-the-pan dopes created by, and then demolished by, our celebrity hyper-focused media. Indeed, the Hollywood celebrity and publicity industry rakes in big bucks by making gods of these mere mortals in the name of stardom. And then it chastises them for being just that: mortal and very fallible.

Most of these folks' troubles, and our nation's, seem to be in California. We all know about the living Jerry Springer show that is Britney Spears' life, but Lindsey Lohan, Hugh Grant, Nick Nolte, Robert Blake, David Hasselhoff, Robert Downey Jr., Alec Baldwin, Al Gore's son, and of course, the celebu-slut Paris Hilton, all have trouble with the law. Nicole Richie was sentenced by the tough L.A. *Law and Order* judge to eighty-two minutes in prison for her drug arrest. It was originally supposed to be four days but the sentencing board felt it was not sending a ridiculous enough message to the kids out there.

Lindsey Lohan had an ankle bracelet on while being arrested this last time from her previous brush with the law over drinking and drugs. Apparently the L.A. courts' ankle bracelets have a built-in GPS system with directions to the nearest liquor store. In addition, there is another breed of celebrity — the politicians. Washington D.C. is just Hollywood for ugly people. This breed is seldom distinguished from actors except that they tend to wear suits with American flag lapel pins. In keeping with my theory about L.A., even the mayor there is in trouble for sleeping with a female reporter. Talk about being screwed by the media! Yet the liberal mayor of L.A. was let off the hook by the president when he was assured it was not a Fox reporter he philandered with.

What is it about that place?

Country music singer Glen Campbell, who many thought was famous enough to be above the law, got arrested in that town recently. He drunkenly totaled his car, was accused of a hit-and-run, fought with the cop, was drunk, and went to jail. On the bright side, the song he writes about it might revive his country music career. If only he could work in something about his dog dying and his momma going to prison then he would have a whole comeback album.

Of all the folks mentioned, the one I have the hardest time with is Paris Hilton. She has done nothing her entire life. She was given about $200 million in a trust fund as a result of the hard work and ingenuity of her grandfather, Baron Hilton, and has simply spent her life being rich. No jobs to speak of (well, she does one type of job), no stress, no car payment, no mortgage, and somehow she finds herself in jail.

How does one screw up being rich? It is not like you are attempting to overthrow a government or perform a heretofore never successful type of brain surgery. All Paris has to do is sit there and be rich, yet she manages to botch that. I guess idle time is indeed the devil's workshop.

Even recently there surfaced another Paris Hilton sex tape — with an hour of footage not in the previous version. Film buffs are excited. It will help critics better piece together the deep meaning of the plots of her previous twenty tapes.

Even beloved Oscar nominee Ryan O'Neal was arrested for drug possession. After his arrest, O'Neal's attorneys said he had legitimate reasons for having so much pot and meth. Now all he has to do is come up with a plausible reason why he bought 5,000 pounds of drugs in an alleyway behind an IHOP from a tattooed man named Cheech.

Chances are the Malibu cops will not get a conviction since all they have is an airtight case against a celebrity. Seemingly the only crime in California a celebrity can commit is saying he or she is a Republican.

At the core of all these drug-driven dopes in L.A. is a rehab center called Promises. It has a revolving door that, if hooked up to a turbine, could provide the energy needs of California for a month. Promises must be one of the few rehab centers with an open bar (their treatment fee is more akin to a cover charge), considering that the results of their fine work can be seen by the constant repeat arrests of stars who spend a night there. Perhaps they should change their name from Promises to Vague Propositions, Questionable Results, Empty Gestures, Enabling Excuses, or Political Campaign Promises.

I think stars may do this whole get-arrested thing to distract the public from what they really have done wrong: their movies. Have you seen a good movie or performance from any of these people ... ever?

I am not sure any of these stars ever really get fixed. In their defense, it is hard to get off booze and drugs when you really do not want to. But at least their antics provide an opportunity for the rest of us to live vicariously without having to go to rehab, prison, or to the Oscars. We should not spend time feeling sorry for such stars; like the rest of us, each person in this country lives in a situation of his or her own making.

"I FORGET—IS LINDSAY LOHAN, PARIS HILTON AND BRITNEY SPEARS SPEEDING WHILE INTOXICATED AND INDECENTLY EXPOSED A `10-87' OR A `10-88'?"

Celebrities Kidding Around

By last count, I have three kids, all teenagers. This is according to contested court rulings and countless DNA tests. Years ago when we contemplated kids, which I had read was a side effect of sex, we went through the normal thought process. We decided to have our own kids, after ruling out my two other proposals, adopting or abducting.

We kept having kids in an attempt to have a good one, and then we just got tired. When they ask, I always tell people that I have two good kids. But then they say, "Don't you have three kids?" I then say, "Yes, but only two are good."

Kids are hard work. Just ask their mother. I sit there and watch her work and realize just how hard raising kids can be. It tires me out to just watch it. Yet the splendor of having these kids makes me think of the fun times. Like when I was single.

Major Hollywood stars go about raising their kids as they do most everything else, by letting others do the work. Having children is so trendy that even minor Hollywood stars have been doing it. Stars choose to adopt rather than risk their bodies and resulting offspring to the vagaries of actually having kids of their own. And instead of children, stars call their kids props.

The hardest part for stars with having kids is coming up with an odd name that some other star has not taken: Apple, Coco, Hazel, Phinnaeus, Prince Michael I and II, George Foreman's 1 through 8, Rumer, Scout, and Moon Unit have all been used. Cher showed us that she has a sense of humor; her kid is named Chastity.

The beat goes on.

Angelina Jolie (who stole Jennifer Aniston's man Brad Pitt when Jennifer was occupied making bad movies), in a feat seldom attempted by a Hollywood starlet, has upped that ante by deciding to deliver an actual child herself. That's why she is a leader in Hollywood. She is willing to try new things.

Remember, she has adopted several kids in her attempt to have one child from every continent. She is starting her own little U.N., but this will be her first real, put-your-body-at-risk baby. I think she ought to give it up for adoption to a Cambodian couple, but I believe she plans to have nannies raise this one too.

The whole issue with Obama not being born in the U.S. is a paranoid right wing conspiracy theory. I cannot believe the right spends so much of its credibility pushing this theory. You can rest assured, if Obama was born in Kenya, Angelina Jolie and Brad Pitt would have attempted to adopt him by now.

Madonna, taking time off from her religion of Kabala and sleeping with young athletes (she has an on-deck circle and a bullpen in her bedroom), is trying to catch up with Angelina. They both love babies, particularly from distant places like Malawi. It is like they are on some kind of baby scavenger hunt. Advantage Angelina.

So many of our stars today are on drugs or incarcerated that it is nice to see a few displaying their own family values. Adoption has been the historic way that starlets get to stage photo ops with their own kids. Tom Cruise and Nicole Kidman adopted several when they were married. When their son was four, he was already taller than Tom. Upon dissolution of their marriage, Nicole not only got to start wearing high heels again, she got to send those kids back to the Paramount Studios prop department.

As these stars get older and tire of looking at themselves in the mirror, some realize that life is not always about themselves. Having kids might be "the ticket," or so say their publicists. The stars can take pictures with them to really connect with America, and then hand them off to the nanny so they can jet off for the next three months to non-union Canada to shoot a movie.

I am not a fan of government intervention, but some authority really needs to look into barring stars from reproducing. I cannot think of one celebrity, except maybe Ronald Reagan, Jr., who has turned out reasonably well adjusted. My feeling is that stars' egos are so big that they do not want to risk children. When you have a child, you in essence, put someone out there who the world knows is yours — mainly because of the last name and court records, so they reflect directly on you.

Their IQ, manners, and success are a direct reflection on you. For this reason, many prefer not to have children, and it is probably for the best.

I love adoption and am glad it is in vogue. I actually have some experience in the area. In high school we adopted a highway. We cleaned it and really grew to love it, but I often wondered, how old does a highway need to be before it is the right time to tell it that it was adopted?

Like with my real kids, you really never know what you should do. I remind my son when he leaves the house that he can be tried as an adult. He is a funny kid, often on the edge of getting by in school. But he is likable. He goes to a school that used to be the Georgia Military Academy, which is where they sent boys before Ritalin.

It is a very structured school, with remnants of tough military-type coaches who tell the kids ad nauseam, "There is no I in team." When my son ran for a class office, his counterculture slogan was, "Elect Jeb, he will put an I in team."

Drunk with success, he ran the next year for class president with the slogan, "Vote for Jeb for Class President. You have seen his grades — he really needs it on his résumé for college."

So maybe I am not the best parent either, but I really look forward to grandparenting, as that it seems much easier. When you are done with them, you just send them back and offer suggestions on how to raise them better. Then you can go back to watching *Matlock*.

There is no accounting for kids and what they do. And the more we wonder why in the world they do the things that they do, we are reminded that we did the same things. You have to have a lot of confidence in yourself to have offspring. They reflect so directly on you, and most of the time, that hurts!

The Super Bowl
Bra-ha-ha

*"One will seldom go wrong in attributing
extreme actions to vanity, moderate ones
to habit, and petty ones to fear."*

— Friedrich Nietzsche

President Bush caught a break last week as the nation's eyes were diverted from WMD intelligence — or lack thereof — and toward the Super Bowl half-time show and Janet Jackson's right breast. While the nation pondered what did the president not know and when did he not know it, Janet knocked this issue off the front page for him.

I am secretly told by a high-ranking source (on the condition that I call him a high-ranking source) that Bush called the New England Patriots after the football game to congratulate the winner, Al Gore called the Panthers to tell them that they were robbed, and Bill Clinton called Janet Jackson.

The sad thing is that even with Janet's pathetic publicity stunt, she is still not the most embarrassing Jackson. Michael switched roles and came to her aid (thus giving Jermaine the day off). A woman's breast, Michael said (and I am not making this up), "is not a sexual thing."

Well, maybe it's not for Michael, but if you get a billion men drinking beer and eating Doritos and then flash something like that, well sir, you got yourself a worldwide Hooters franchise.

After we all fought our way through commercials about erectile dysfunction and a flatulent Budweiser horse, we get to the wholesome halftime show. I am thinking, "Maybe a nice Punt, Pass and Kick competition," but no. We get nasty lyrics from rappers who scratched themselves as if they needed crotch powder, Kid Rock in an American flag poncho and the like. I am thinking it can't get any worse. Then, Janet Jackson comes out and does this clearly rehearsed bit with Justin Timberlake, who took some much needed time off from "Bringing Sexy Back."

Afterward, Justin tried to make himself out to be the victim. What male among us has not felt violated shortly after ripping a girl's top off? This was not just another case of an innocent young boy being taken advantage of by a Jackson. It was ten years before neighbors of Michael Jackson's Neverland Ranch realized that it was not a middle-school for boys.

Even at the Grammys, Justin still feigned contrition, and the U.S. pretended to be offended. Madonna was raging about censorship and defended Justin. I can always tell when Madonna is angry — she slips out of her fake British accent.

This is a simple and age-old formula: Men like boobs. A funny quote, and this could never be spoken by a world leader today, was from Winston Churchill. Well into retirement, he went to Birmingham, England, for an unveiling of a statue of him. Two pretty hostesses gushed over him and told him how they "had traveled from Liverpool for this unveiling of his bust." He looked at them and said, "Be assured, ladies, I would do the same for you."

I long for the creative and subtle remarks like Churchill's that would, sadly, end a politician's career in the PC world of today. Yet, Janet's crass move will elevate her dying career. Just as MTV was compiling old footage of her for a "Where are They Now" segment, she does this "tit for tat" stunt, and she is back on top! Sad commentary.

Outraged by Janet's Teat Offensive, the nation's media, which have always protected the delicate sensibilities of us town folks, feigned their outrage. So worried that kids may have seen this, they replayed the three-second event in slow motion 17,000 times a day just to reinforce to us their heartfelt concern — for the kids of course, not their ratings.

In the media's defense, and again proving that they are not a monolithic monopoly, news agencies covered this in different ways. Some covered her breast with a gray blob, others with a black patch, and still others — displaying cutting-edge technology — chose to Pixelate it. Diversity of coverage is always their goal.

The media stood principled as always and sent a clear and stern message that there is a price to pay for lowbrow antics like Janet's (Miss Jackson if you're nasty), and that price is tons of free media coverage that will resuscitate her otherwise dead career. Her career was about to be featured on *Cold Case Files* when this Hail Mary was tossed. Take that! CBS, whose executives also were "appalled by this and taken by surprise," (wink-wink) announced a shake-up. The ten executives responsible for this were summarily brought into corporate, browbeaten by Andy Rooney, (that has to hurt) then promoted.

And the Bush administration had the FCC immediately start an investigation.

The committee to look into why we went to war (which I have been against as a Libertarian) because of faulty intelligence will take a year or so to get cranking (the report is expected right after the fall election, oddly enough), but they are getting their hands on this boob thing pronto.

This whole bra-ha-ha has caused the Jackson family patriarch, Slappin' Joe Jackson, to rethink his estranged family's strategy. Since all Jackson 5 kids have moved far away, Joe was saddened by the fact that there was no Jackson family member he could immediately slap around. But always the practical administrator of the Jackson family business, Joe did say that if either Michael or Janet had to serve jail time over recent charges, he would send Tito in their place.

Ministers Should Do More Than Lay People

(The Reverend Ted Haggard story)

"Men never do evil so completely and cheerfully as when they do it from a religious conviction."

— Blaise Pascal, 17th-century French mathematician,
philosopher and physicist

My great-grandfather was a Methodist minister in the South. He had a sense of humor and his rural congregants loved him. A parishioner suggested he ask God for rain to relieve a drought. He told the farmer that he would if he could, but he was in sales, not operations.

It seems today that the era of the humble minister is long gone, to be replaced by televangelists and megachurch "charismatics" who are all business. Many of them take themselves very seriously, are overtly political, and do not lead by example. As a result, they seem to be losing touch with their followers, who are not zealots. Truly, religion has been Swaggared, Haggared, and Bakkered of late, and as a result, trivialized. And this doesn't count the priest who ex-Foley-ated a future congressman on a boys' camping trip.

The flameout of the Rev. Ted Haggard, the disgraced former head of the National Association of Evangelicals and founding pastor of a 14,000-member Colorado Springs megachurch, is emblematic of the problems facing contemporary evangelical churches.

These huge churches choose their pastors based on charisma, marketing sense, and the ability to be trusted with sensitive personal information. It's much the same way Tom Cruise picks a wife.

After denying that he ever met the gay escort who says he had a three-year relationship with him, Rev. Ted finally confessed. Before I cast the first stone, what man among us has not summoned a gay male prostitute to our hotel room for a massage and to score a little methamphetamine with church money? You talk about robbing Paul to pay for Peter!

President Bush, always using government to impose his religious social values, pressed for a constitutional amendment banning gay marriage. Most in Congress feel that the only way two men should be in bed with each other is if one is a lobbyist with campaign cash and the other is a congressman up for reelection. Clearly they need to spend their time forbidding two retired lesbian gym teachers from Kansas from opening up joint checking accounts. Having caught Osama Bin Laden and done such a great job on the deficit, we should allow Congress to meddle in this important national issue that could harm so many of us.

Apparently, by pushing the ban, Bush believes that two people who want to commit to a monogamous relationship should not be allowed to, thus ensuring that gay guys are made to have sex with as many other anonymous gay guys as humanly possible. Good news for the San Francisco bath house business and airport bathrooms nationwide!

We are clearly on a national march toward gay marriage of some kind. I hope it continues state by state rather than with a national mandate (pun intended). Clearly gays will not be happy until they are treated like the rest of us and allowed to be miserable in marriage. Some day gay marriage will be as common as an NFL player arrest. Wedding planners across the fruited plains will be able to plan their own wedding some day. And, in what might stem their desire for marriage, come to know the eternal joy of giving someone a house and paying alimony.

In fact California briefly allowed gays to get married — which will mark the first time a gay man was allowed to marry where Liza Minnelli was not the bride. Then, when gays were later not allowed to marry they pitched a hissy fit and marched on the L.A. courthouse in anger. Some estimates are that the gay men did some $5 million in decorating improvement during the protest march.

Politicians seem to feel like they cannot fight for gay marriage. Even Hillary Clinton, the Wellesley woman in comfortable pantsuits, has been called a "disappointment on same-sex marriage" by lesbian groups. Bill Clinton came to her defense by saying, to be fair, she is equally disappointing on opposite-sex marriage.

I really do not see why Hillary is not at least for civil unions. It allows couples to live together for mutual benefit in an arrangement that is not a true marriage by traditional norms, but fulfills the needs and ambitions of both partners to coexist and achieve. You know, like Hillary and Bill's marriage.

So back to Rev. Ted. If society was easier on this issue and there were not so many antiquated Biblical cross currents on it, men like Rev. Ted would not have to conceal their sexuality. It hurts the wife (exposing her to sexual diseases) and their kids. It will be interesting to see how Ted Haggard plays this one. I have my theory on it.

My guess is that Rev. Ted plays the fake addiction card and goes to drunk camp for about thirty days, then comes out all cured of his gayness and ready to preach again or play a victim on TV. There is nothing the pious like to do more than to forgive someone, as it makes them feel superior. This is often the motivation for forgiveness.

Sadly, there are a few who pray on their knees on Sunday and then prey on others all week. And in my view, there is no bigger crime than to gain someone's trust using the fear of God, then to take advantage of the vulnerable. These folks have a special place in Hell reserved for them, right next to Hitler and the guy who invented the low-flow showerhead.

If you are going to set out lofty goals for your flock, you have to be an example to them. The harm done by these few men of the loincloth do untold damage to organized religion, which will continue to lose ground.

Churches have done so much good for so many over the years. They are there to relieve human anxiety, comfort the afflicted, and provide a sense of community. It is human nature to want to be loved, and some are even willing to join a quasi hate group to get it. Yet it is equally wrong for liberals to vilify all churchgoers as dumb white trash, devoid of reason. I guess "judgment day" will determine who is right.

What makes Rev. Ted a national story is the hypocrisy that stems from his fight to keep gays from wedlock. He does not even want gay men to be wedding planners. His best chance to get out of hot water with the other evangelicals is by making the case that he just slept with a dude — he did not marry him.

It has been my experience that men who spend an inordinate amount of time bashing gays often have insecurities that they are fighting, bubbling very near the surface. Secure men, while we do not like to think about the mechanics of gay sex, do not persecute gays. I do not care what a gay guy does, as long as he does not try to do it to me. And if a man somehow fears a gay guy might rape him, then he really is not much of a man. Two consenting gay guys antiquing in Vermont do not harm anyone, so let's focus on what matters in government: Congress spending our children's future away in wasteful self-indulgent projects.

I have to conclude that gays must be pre-wired as homosexual. Folks, you just don't catch gay. A virus did not cause Richard Simmons or Little Richard. So, since God is responsible for the pre-wiring, how can that be so damnable if done between consenting adults? If He made them that way, then the Christian logic would follow that they, too, are people of God. When they react with such hate, it makes me wonder just what sort of Christians they are.

Not only are churches becoming more political, they now aggressively teach sexual abstinence. When I was growing up they never taught such a thing, as folks in my church would have blushed even talking about it. The way I learned abstinence was the old-fashioned way: dating a Catholic girl.

Perhaps these ministers need to practice what they preach on abstinence, avoid politics, and be more like my great-granddad. If the Crystal Meth-odist Rev. Ted outing taught us anything, it is that it is more embarrassing to be a hypocrite than a gay male hooker. As Rev. Ted found out, you can't have your gay pretty boys and persecute them too.

Make a Joyful Noise to the Judge

*"Religion is excellent stuff for keeping
the common people quiet."*

— Napoleon Bonaparte

Two of the great thinkers of our nation have something else in common.

Both Michael Vick and Paris Hilton have found religion, after being faced with jail time for making another in a series of bad decisions based on their delusions of infallibility. With the plague of all these famous people going through such tribulations, I believe the Old Testament says that we are in for locusts next.

Just last week, Michael Vick performed his lawyer-written mea culpa after pleading guilty to federal crimes — oddly the same crimes that one week ago he denied doing — during which he said, "Through this situation I found Jesus and asked him for forgiveness and turned my life over to God."

In an awkward moment, his agent, Joel Segal, chimed in and reminded him that he still gets his 10 percent before God gets his.

Vick, having played the race card, (which got trumped by the reality card), chose to try religious conversion, the guilty person's fallback standard, to garner sympathy from the public and, more importantly, the sentencing judge.

I am no legal scholar and have only seen a few episodes of *Matlock*, but I do think famous people have the right to a publicist. If they cannot afford one, the court should be required to provide one. I believe this was decided in the landmark indigent celebrity case of *Nick Nolte v. California of 2005*.

Religion has long been used by those in trouble who should have known better. This was even the case with Paris Hilton, who could have gone with rehab, ever the favorite Hollywood fallback option. Drunk camp of the stars, Promises Rehab in L.A. even has temporary parking spots out front for the celebs in a hurry to go through the motions. Instead, and always the L.A. trendsetter, Paris claimed to have read the Bible and turned her life around during her twenty-three days in prison.

She told her L.A. following that "she had found God in prison." And after they asked, "What He was in for?" the L.A. media realized that she was talking about the Bible and Christianity, this thing that Mel Gibson ran with all the way to the bank in *The Passion of the Christ*. They vowed to look into it, but could not find a Bible at any store in L.A.

Recently, Senator David Vitter, another "Family Values" Republican from Louisiana, played the religion card after he got busted hiring Washington D.C. hookers. He told his constituents something to the effect that he had resolved his actions with his God. Now, unless his God is Charlie Sheen, my guess is that this kind of reconciliation is going to take more than a press conference.

More troubling to me as a Libertarian, Vitter said that he often would pay the prostitute and just talk to her instead of having sex. I view this as just another alarming example of government waste, and I find it even more troubling than his hooker problem.

Vick, Paris, and Vitter are simply following a pattern set by other infamous criminals like Manuel Noriega, who had the chutzpah to stage his baptism in the courthouse, Oklahoma City bomber Terry Nichols, and countless others who have feigned religion to play to a sympathetic and forgiving Christian public.

The real truth is not that they say they have changed their lives in and around jail time, it is what they do afterward that matters. The only person I can think of who really seemed sincere about finding God was Watergate's Charles Colson, who set up and continued working for Prison Fellowship, the ministry he founded in jail. Perhaps Paris could found Skanks for God. Or maybe she has done enough for religion already by disproving the theory of "intelligent design" with her every action.

Religion has long been used by many to divert attention or explain misdeeds, usually only when convenient or spoken to a public made gullible by the belief that somehow this person's God has made amends with the transgression. Congressmen to car dealers have used the pretense of religion to sell something of questionable value to a proletariat of believers in America. To me, it is overused and has gotten old. It has bought too many passes for people undeserving, and confused on the issues of good and bad for way too many years.

When all these thugs and dopes try to come into court with the Bible acting like they have turned their lives around somewhere between their conviction and sentencing, I would do what one of my favorite judges does. When a heinous criminal shows up in court with a Bible, this judge always asks the toter of the Good Book if he knows where the Apostle Paul was when he wrote most of the books of the New Testament.

Invariably the defendant does not know.

The judge then bangs the gavel and says, "Paul was in jail, and I am going to give you the same opportunity that he had!"

Eliot Mess — Spitzer Swallows and the Audacity of a Dope

It's when things like this happen that I love writing this column. If you have read my past work (and I don't blame you if you have not, as I find it a bit locker room and boorish), you would know how I feel about Eliot Spitzer. He represents the ambitious politician who will ruin anyone he can for his own self-serving reason to gain elected status. He is the classic Ayn Rand government figure who is egotistical and maniacal. So egotistical, in fact, that he was upset with only being Client 9 and was feverishly working to be Client 1 of that call-girl business.

It is rumored that Spitzer might go to prison for this and he may not like it — there he will not have to pay for sex. If Karma has its way, Eliot Spitzer's cellmate may do to him what he and like-minded politicians have been doing to citizens for years.

I will not point out the obvious of how the holier-than-thou types who judge others harshly are the ones always caught in such hypocrisy. It is Shakespearean and will repeat itself in the future. Like most, I really feel for his wife, a nice Southern Baptist woman from Concord, North Carolina, and his three girls. I do not, however, feel sorry for him, and anyone who has known Spitzer would agree.

When I wrote about him negatively in the past, I was always fearful that he would call a press conference to say that he was indicting me for late Blockbuster fees or the impure thoughts I harbor about Sarah Palin. The power that prosecuting attorneys have in America to go after whom they want, often for personal political gain, needs to be addressed.

I am reminded of a story my cousin told me after graduating from the University of Virginia School of Law. He was a policeman and fought as a Marine in the first Iraq invasion. He told me about a U.S. attorney who claimed he could indict whoever he wanted and do whatever he wanted, and uttered those famous words that should strike fear in all of us: "I could indict a ham sandwich if I wanted to."

The unchecked populist ego of Spitzer, who seemed to love ruining the lives of innocent and well-intentioned champions of industry for sport, is what got him thinking that he was above the law. This makes him a great Democrat and earned him consideration as a possible running mate for Hillary. She can pick her men! Politically, Hillary can no longer run with him, but she is probably more inclined to marry him now.

One thing we have learned here and with the Duke lacrosse "rape" case brought by fellow Democrat and selective prosecution aficionado, Mike Nifong, is that prosecutors should not be allowed to run for office. Nifong did resign from public office so he could devote more time to making up stories and ruining kids lives in the private sector.

And yes, Rudy Giuliani took on high profile cases, but at least he had the guts to take on the mob.

Spitzer clearly likes risks, so much so that he had a hooker tell him what he wanted to do was "dangerous." When a prostitute tells you you are out of line, dude, you are out there. He wanted to do it without protection. Sleeping with a hooker without a condom is much like bungee jumping — if the rubber breaks you are dead.

Knowing he did not wear a condom has to really make it a little slice of heaven for his wife.

It has never even occurred to me to hire a hooker, mainly because I am cheap and do not want to pay to disappoint a woman when I can do that for free. But I do have acquaintances that enjoy paying for "sexual favors," as they call it. I always respond that it is technically not a favor if you pay for it; it is more like a contractual obligation. The only reasonable explanation that I have ever gotten from a busy rich guy who fancies the call girls was when I asked him why he paid for a hooker to come over for an hour. He looked at me and said, "Ron, I do not pay for them to come over. The money is paid so they will leave." Yet in all of this, it reminds us that there is no limit to the male ego and the ensuing hubris that comes with perceived power. From such a severe and unfeeling man who would hurt another human being just so he would get TV coverage, it is no surprise that he could detach himself from intimacy and enjoy violating a prostitute for his own enjoyment.

Added to this problem was that people feared the wrath of Spitzer should they take him to task.

Spitzer was given way too much good press by the liberal media for selective prosecution for years. The media love the populist persecution of business because it feeds their class-envy model of how they influence the poor and less educated to vote for Democrats. If you vilify business and aggrandize government, you fulfill your vision of a more centrally run economy. Jobs and businesses just leave our country as a result, but they never make that cause-and-effect connection.

The main point of what happens when we are unfriendly to businesses with litigation, overregulation, and taxes is that they simply go to another country. That is why London is becoming the financial capital of the world. In recent years, eighteen of the twenty biggest stock offerings were done on the London exchange when, in previous years, they would have gone public on the New York Stock Exchange. That, my friends, is a scary trend. You cannot chase businesses out of the country like that.

When populist politicians gain power by vilifying the people who are the economic engine of our once-capitalistic economy, we are in for a downward spiral in America that really frightens me. I hope it scares you, too.

Justice Antonin Scalia and The Supremes

"Whatever it is that the government does, sensible Americans would prefer that the government does it to somebody else. This is the idea behind foreign policy."

— P. J. O'Rourke

Recently a board that I serve on in Washington, D.C., had the privilege of having a small meeting with Supreme Court Justice Antonin Scalia. It may come as no surprise to you all that I was before a judge again, but this time it was cool.

Scalia is a famous jurist, admired for his intellect and convictions by many, and hated by liberals for his willingness to act on his convictions. I admire him for his courage, as he regularly hunts with Dick Cheney. No matter the form of admiration or contempt that you might have for this man, it is probably entirely media-driven.

Since "The Supremes" rarely defend themselves when attacked, the liberal media, comedians, and the like have been able to take cheap shots at this man for years. The media will make anyone they choose out to be as bad as they desire by controlling the narrative. And, having heard all those stories about him, I, too, was braced for a brazen, cantankerous man, full of hubris and conceit. The man we met was nothing like that and actually quite the opposite.

Coming from an Italian immigrant family, Antonin Scalia graduated valedictorian of his Georgetown University class in 1957. That was back before professors gave those guilt A's to students they felt had been wronged.

He then went on to Harvard Law and taught at University of Virginia Law School. He is the embodiment of the American Dream, and to have been so maligned by the press during his tenure on the Court is a travesty.

He came out to speak to us, and I thought Danny DeVito was playing the role of Judge Scalia that day. He was a sensible, down-to-earth man who you would feel very comfortable making major decisions for you.

When asked whether he had been a difficult judge who did not get along with other judges, he told us that (contrary to media opinion) his best friend on the court is Ruth Bader Ginsberg. You all know Judge Ginsberg — she was the hottest chick in the court until Anna Nicole Smith came before them last week with her divorce case.

You would think that a former stripper and gold digger like Anna Nicole would have been uncomfortable in the Supreme Court, but remember — she has spent a lot of time around old men in robes in her day!

After Bush messed up by trying to appoint Harriet Miers, a never-married/no-boyfriend woman whom many viewed as too liberal, to the Supreme Court, he is scrambling to correct his miscalculation. He hid his faux pas by declaring that he had directed NASA to have a man on Miers by 2009. He then said she had "done a heckuva" job and went back to nicknaming the White House press corp.

Scalia spoke openly and humbly about the court, history, and the role the justices play. The impression that I got was that he wishes more judges/lawyers had other jobs like carpenters, factory workers, and the like, as every major decision that they make comes down to their sense of right and wrong. Being a lawyer does not automatically endow a person with a strong sense of right and wrong, only a sense of what one can get away with under the law.

My sense is that the "conservative judges" feel strongly that the less that is decided on the federal level, the better for all of us. The media paints these guys as Nazi-like old fogies who want to limit your rights and, with only short notice, might even outlaw dancing if given a chance in a case like the *Rev. Falwell v. Footloose*. Nothing could be further from the truth. These judges believe in individual freedom and liberty, unfettered by government intervention.

And on that note, and following up on what I have said in the past, he also feels that students should read *The Federalist Papers*. Of course, public schools would never make kids read this work as it speaks to limited government and personal responsibility. Teachers unions want none of that.

In any political discussion, or upon reading a column like mine that takes sides, people get emotional. We have to realize that on any issue about which reasonable folks can have a reasonable difference of opinion, we should not personalize it to the point of anger.

If a liberal makes a logical case in an e-mail to me about one of my columns, I would rather discuss that with him than a ditto-head who agrees with me. In the rare case the former happens, I really enjoy the debate and value that argument. I imagine this is how Scalia feels and would hope that our Supreme Court does as well.

As an aside, the one demographic that I find odd as a Southerner is that there are few of us on the Supreme Court. For some reason Northerners find their way to that venue to argue important cases. Perhaps because they seem to like to argue more than we more genteel Southerners. Being raised an Italian in New York, I am sure Scalia honed his debating skills in the landmark 1985 case of *Hey You Freakin' Lookin at Me? v. Yeah, I am, What of It?*

By permission of Michael Ramirez and Creators Syndicate, Inc.

It seems that the political discourse in this country is getting meaner, (much of it between George Bush and Ted Kennedy who never seemed to get along after they stopped drinking) and issues do not seem to be vetted fairly. Scalia, the judge most hated by the left, was confirmed ninety-eight to zero in 1986. Imagine how he would fare today.

An open and factual exchange of ideas helps us all make better decisions. And remember, this man has hunted with Cheney and lived to talk about it. You cannot hurt him with words in the press!

Family, Friends, and Football

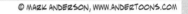

A Family Affair

*"I'd rather laugh with the sinners
than cry with the saints."*

— Billy Joel, "Only the Good Die Young"

I just got back from my annual family reunion, and like most families, we have our share of characters that make you wonder if you are really related to them folks. I have long said that I come from an uncomfortable mixture of MIT graduates and drywall hangers. The odd thing is it has taken 20 years for my wife to figure out which is which — as there is often a very thin line between the two.

Like most American families, the older generation has sacrificed and seen to it that their kids have done better than themselves. I will not bore you with the relatives that are lawyers, financial officers, Apache helicopter pilots serving in Iraq, etc., because it is always more interesting to talk about the scoundrels and scallywags.

Therefore I will focus on my favorite Uncle Mac. Imagine the character Uncle Rico from the movie *Napoleon Dynamite*. Mac is part huckster, clown, alley cat, and 100 percent American. He works hard in construction yet is always broke. Not M.C. Hammer- or Willie Nelson-post-lRS-problems-broke mind you, but he barely gets by. Sadly, his dream job was never realized. He has long said that he really wanted to be a door-to-door gynecologist.

Mac arrived at our house, and it was with mixed emotions that I let my 16-year-old son unload his car. Mac drinks only Budweiser now and arrived with three cases. He instructed my son to put the ice on his beer in his Igloo cooler so as to properly prepare his "medicine chest." He told my son, "You know, I don't even like the taste, it is just that my doctors insist I drink it."

He proceeded to the screened-in porch and commenced drinking and telling stories for forty-eight hours. He recounted stories of the other scoundrels in the family and regaled us with tales (both real and imagined) that had us laughing with tears streaming down our faces almost all day. Many of the stories are about my grandfather, whom we all loved, that ended up making us both laugh and cry.

Mac is a good man, on balance, who tells folks that he was drafted, then shot during Vietnam. This is technically true. He got drafted, and before he left for basic training got into a bar fight over a woman, and the guy shot him in the knee while trying to make him dance by shooting a .22 rifle at his feet. So he never served our country in any official capacity. If he had, I am not sure his service would have altered the outcome of that war. But I am sure that he would still have been shot, either by the Vietcong or his fellow soldiers.

Mac is not exactly a man of letters. When asked where he went to college he will say "Penn State." Then, invariably, the person who asks the question will pause with astonishment, and he will say, "Oh wait, or was it the State Pen?"

He probably had the IQ to do well in school had they only had Ritalin back then. Lots and lots of Ritalin. When he first starting drinking, a lifetime avocation, he said he liked to drink Jim Beam bourbon, because the square bottle was less likely to roll underneath his feet when he was stopped by the cops. He is an accomplished drinker, and to my knowledge has never had a DUI.

Perhaps his cunning kept him from a DUI and from ever harming anyone. His favorite bar is next to a Domino's Pizza. After a hard night of drinking at the bar he would simply call Domino's next door and order a pizza for home delivery. In 10 minutes he would go next door and jump in the car with the delivery boy, exchange pleasantries and ride home with him. The ride would cost him $10 and he would have a pizza when he got home.

He still misses his dog, a small Chihuahua he named Rambo who he is convinced died of AIDS. But since he lives on a small farm, he has plenty of animals. In fact, he says he has the only place where, when the pound comes out, they have to call for back-up.

After the weekend I felt the need to apologize to my kids, but then I thought better of it. Genes not only give one his or her physical appearance but they also give descendants their predispositions to various vices, brilliance, humor, and goodness. It is my hope that the virtues carry the day and, at a minimum, we can all laugh. And yet, family is the cheapest form of human pleasure that we all have, especially if it is nurtured and not taken too seriously.

Inoculating Kids

"I like to instruct people. It is noble to teach oneself. It is still nobler to teach others, and less trouble."

— Mark Twain

It is with trepidation that I set about sending my oldest to college. Years of my 100 percent right wing indoctrination could possibly be vetoed by a dreamy, idealistic, and charismatic professor in a turtleneck. And, make no mistake; they are out there just waiting to wipe out all the values that I have instilled in my kids. But I must let go, and let the child leave the nest to test her resolve in the crazy world we, for some reason, call "higher education."

Stories abound of college students ridiculed by professors in class when they stake out conservative positions on matters. Papers that should be given an A somehow get a B- when the position is contrary to that of the liberal professor. It happened to me, and it will happen to our kids.

It is interesting that college campuses, which espouse "diversity," are the least tolerant of opposing ideas. Professors know that they have one shot at kids, probably at their most vulnerable time, to transform them into liberals.

Liberal thinking works only in the theoretical world of academia, where it goes virtually unchecked by administrators under the guise of academic freedom and tenure. Liberals are drawn to teaching, much like men with a predisposition to show their butt crack become plumbers.

The old saying, "Those who can, do; those who cannot, teach." (and I think those who can do neither, teach gym) holds true here. This is not to say that there are not some great fair and balanced professors in college; I had several whom I still speak to frequently. But the latest polls that I have read indicate that a large majority are Democrats and many are militant liberals who, fortified with tenure, seek to advance their "vision."

The lack of intellectual diversity seems to endanger the very purpose of college. As it has for ages, people who gravitate toward that profession are of the same ilk. Like-minded folks tend to gravitate toward similar professions, and that is fine with me. You could have knocked me over with his feathering scissors when I found out my daughter's hair stylist, Brian, was gay.

My biggest fear is that I will raise a brat. I have always remembered a great story I was told about a man from Boston who went into a Waffle House in Atlanta. He went to the counter, met a guy and asked him his name. The guy responded and the Bostonian asked him to spell his name as he filled out the back of a car title. The Atlanta man said, "What are you doing?" He said, "I am giving you my daughter's car." "What?" said the man receiving the car.

The man from Boston went on to explain that his Wellesley College grad, who has never been grateful for anything that he had done for her, called from Atlanta. The 28-year-old girl was following the Grateful Dead around and her car broke down. In a bitchy tone she called her dad for the first time in three weeks and said in an angry voice, "My car is broken down in Atlanta; what are you going to do about it?" The Bostonian sadly looked at the man at the Waffle House as he handed him the title to the car and said, "This is what I am doing about it."

He lamented letting his kid fell prey to the elite college sense of entitlement and anger over historic events that never even happened to her, and told the man not to let it happen to him. I have never forgotten that story.

I am always amazed that we entrust our kids to colleges that are so opposite to our own values. Since the elite colleges are in fact a monopoly, (by this I mean you could not re-create a Harvard from scratch), they should be held more accountable. The major drift is so far to the left, so far out of the mainstream that when former president of Harvard Larry Summers made the empirical statement women's math scores are a bit lower than men's, he was chased around the ivy towers like he was Hitler.

Where has common sense gone? Are these colleges stuck on stupid? Education, as dispensed by these tenured liberal nut jobs, and the rate at which they raise tuition, makes me wonder if it is worth it. Clearly, we have to trust that we have fortified our kids against all of the college experience, including drinking and drugs. We know that kids are malleable and eager to please at that age.

We have to protect our kids against the evils of corporate America. My youngest was looking forward to getting her first summer job and went to an interview. She came home upset and almost in tears. She said that the guy she interviewed with asked her first thing if she could make coffee. Even I found that wrong, and I am a pro-business chauvinist. Then she fought back a smile and said, "Yeah Dad, that is the last time I apply to work at that Caribou Coffee shop."

Buying into the liberal mindset is easy because liberals are for everything and against nothing. It is easy being a liberal and espousing the liberal doctrine, whose sole purpose is to always make you feel good about yourself. We ought to give more to the poor, house the homeless, pay the unions more, give more money to Third World countries, forgive their debts, etc. It is easy to be for something that you do not have to pay for. Liberals are for all expenses paid for with someone else's money. The hard thing is to stand strong against frivolous things, when it is so easy just to say that you are for them — then just go smoke some weed. So teachers should just teach.

Math teachers should not say, "One plus one equals two — and, oh yeah, Bush lied." I will tell my daughter it is senseless to try to talk facts and logic to folks who are drunk with their sense of moral superiority.

Yet, I am not in agreement with the far right that wants to regulate this. The best way to change this is not through a Tom Delay-type legislative move, but through a good-faith effort by colleges to self-regulate. If not, then we should stop sending our kids, and our money, to such schools.

It seems ironic that the "best" colleges have the most liberal teachers. Further irony is that the endowments of these schools are funded by mostly conservative business people. There is a point at which those and others of us must take a firm stand on this issue.

I would do it, but I just got a foot massager for Christmas and will be quite busy until I tire of it, most likely about mid-February.

Let Children Discover Life On Own Terms

At some point, our village elders decided that a boy becomes an adult at 18. I am convinced this was determined by folks who had never met any 18-year-olds.

My son leaves for college this week, and I have to learn to temper my expectations both for his grades and his tenure at his chosen institution of higher learning. He started early with summer school, a strategy adopted by colleges to steer kids away from actually working at a summer job. Too much reality detracts from the soft theoretical la-la land of college. My son battled me so much all through high school that I threatened to send him to military school. And not a good one either, but one of those that has to advertise at the back of *Southern Living* magazine.

There is this built-in societal pressure for parents to ride kids hard to make good grades, and I wonder if we are not just driving both ourselves and the kids nuts by doing so. Kids have to have a light on and want to learn something. It is at that point they get interested and absorb information they seek out themselves. Certainly it is not having to read Chaucer.

We probably overeducate many kids in the United States, well beyond their interest in school and, in many cases, their abilities. The reality is that college is just a place to store a kid in the hope that he or she grows up by the time they are done. They learn many life lessons there, such as how much liquor they can hold and how to pay speeding and parking tickets.

My son took a less difficult route than my daughter. She is at Vanderbilt. He felt that he wanted to go to a big state SEC school, and our state, which is 49th in education, was a bit ambitious, so he went to Ole Miss for college — securely the 50th-ranked state and on a par with Washington D.C. and Guam.

He is leaving nothing to chance by letting hard classes get in the way of his college experience. At his age, some kids drink from the fountain of knowledge, but he will only gargle and spit it out — probably on a fraternity pledge.

On the bright side, he does have some college goals in mind aside from dressing well and dating many coeds. He said that Ole Miss was ranked the fifth-best party school, yet he felt strongly that he and the few kids going over with him from his high school could quickly get it to number three.

Since Ole Miss is a party school, his first move will be to abolish tuition in favor of just a cover charge each semester. Pay it, they stamp your hand, and you are good to go.

As those of us who went to universities can attest, most of a student's education occurs outside of the classroom. And with the tenured ultra-liberal professors harbored on today's campuses, that is a good thing. As parents, we risk entrusting these malleable minds to these teachers who have strong liberal opinions on everything, including where their coffee beans are grown. Yet, Ole Miss is not as bad as most colleges; I understand it has one professor who voted for a Republican once.

As parents, we have to let our children go and discover life on their own terms. By 18, the die is probably cast. My son's view seems to be that the sooner he gets behind in school, the more time he has to catch up. It will be fun to see if this pans out for him in college.

A friend reminded me of a scene from *Sanford and Son*, one of my favorite shows when I was growing up. The father, Fred Sanford, said to his son Lamont, "Didn't you learn anything from being my son? What do you think I'm doing this all for?"

Lamont Sanford answered, "Yourself." Fred said, "Yeah, you learned something."

Parents who push their kids too hard are doing it for themselves and not for the kid. Like any successful endeavor, one has to want to do it on one's own. All we can hope is to keep our kids positive and safe until that light comes on someday and they find something that they really want to pursue. And it is rarely what we parents had in mind.

Sex, Lies, Statistics

*"A promiscuous person is someone
getting more sex than you are."*

— Victor Lownes, *Playboy* executive

For those of us who have teenage kids, it was nice to read that a recent survey by our own Department of Health and Human Services said that 15- to 17- year-olds are having less sex. The most recent survey said 30 percent of teenage girls have had sex, down from 38 percent in 1995 (the Clinton years). Apparently the Clinton administration knew of this and did nothing about it. I think Congress should spend our tax dollars to investigate.

In the study, girls cited religious and moral reasons for waiting. So religion does do more than rationalize wars! The second reason was fear of pregnancy and diseases. These reasons were followed closely by "boys are icky."

This was good news for me, because two of my three children are girls. As a father, all I really have to do is to make sure my daughters don't end up on the brass pole with some stage name like Ambrosia or Mercedes.

Growing up awkwardly in a small town, I had built-in defenses from having sex, not the least of which was that girls would have nothing to do with me. That severely limits a young man's options. If asked, and FYI — because of a more polite society — there were no surveys taken back then on matters such as these, I am sure I would have checked the "moral concerns" box. When in doubt and unsuccessful, always stake out the moral high ground. It gives you solace and it confuses and confounds your inquirer.

It would be hard for a boy who was 138 pounds of bones and asthma to do anything anyway, even in a small town with little else to do. My sex life was seemingly an endless series of trial and error. The cold reality when you were like me — remember I could not make a fist until I was 19 — was that the "early bloomers" (the guys who failed a grade) were the real pioneers in this area. We would sit around the locker room and listen to a fifth-year junior tell us about his exploits, both real and imagined. Both types of stories kept us spellbound.

With my boy I have to take a different tack. Long ago I got comfortable with the double standard of men and women as it relates to sex, bathrooms, wedding planning, empathy, thank-you notes, and the truth. The double standard works both ways, so do not think me a chauvinist. For example, if a man talks dirty to woman, it is sexual harassment. If a woman talks dirty to a man, it is $6.99 a minute.

There is a statistic that 90 percent of college-aged men and 43 percent of women have had sex. Now, just doing some simple math here, either some women or men are lying, or there are a handful of women who are very, very busy.

My observation of men and women and romance, while not entirely scientific, is as follows. Women seem to need to have a reason to have sex; men just seem to need a place. Genders are wired differently, and the sooner we acknowledge that, the better we all are. The dude touched on it with *Women are from Mars and Men are at the Bar*, or something like that. But having three teenagers would be really, really fun if it were not happening to me. I can't have candid conversations with them, as I tend to make jokes. It lessens the experience.

Like millions of other fathers around the country, I avoid the subject in hopes that it never comes up again. If I were not a parent I would like to tell them about love, which I believe is the sweetest and most wholesome thing two or more people can enjoy. So you can see why my family and the various child services departments with open files on me forbid me talking to kids about such matters.

Yet raising my kids has been a pleasure. It makes me appreciate the simple things in life, like being alone.

However, parents must soldier on, and we find happiness in other parents' stories about their adolescents. I am reminded of a buddy in New York, a tough Italian guy who was a trader of stocks at my old firm, and his attempt to talk to his son about sex. He lamented to me one day about his 15-year-old son, little Tony, who was "no longer master of his domain." His wife was bustin' his chops to talk to little Tony about, and I have to paraphrase here, his natural curiosity at that age. Big Tony put it off for weeks. I would ask him if he had had "*the* conversation with little Tony" and he would get ticked off. He dreaded it so much.

So one day his wife called and said, "I am having to deal with this all the time, and you need to come home, be a man, and have that talk with little Tony." Big Tony sat little Tony down that night and awkwardly stumbled through his rehearsed opening line, "Your momma says you are doing this, and I am your father and am here to tell you not to."

There was a pause and little Tony's eyes got big as he was naturally curious about sex and was seizing on the opportunity to discuss it with his dad. Little Tony asked, "Dad have you ever done it?"

Big Tony was shell-shocked; he had not anticipated the question. Yet he did not want to appear a hypocrite at this critical father-son moment and blurted out, "No, absolutely not."

Little Tony's eyes look downward, and then he looked up at his Dad with a smile and said, "Dad, you really have to try this!"

Best to Say Nothing

No side will win the Battle of the Sexes. There's
too much fraternizing with the enemy.

— Henry Kissinger

I have long said that we men really are not much. Women are unquestionably the superior gender. We certainly would not be at war now in Iraq if women were in charge.

My son, who is embarking on that stage of his life where he is thinking about a wife, recently asked me a few questions about women. With all the divorces we have, including Heather Mills' recent award of $50 million for her marriage to Paul McCartney, it is a good subject. Heather's settlement amounts to $1,400 an hour for her marriage, which the judge was able to easily value based on the prices Eliot Spitzer paid.

It occurred to me that I really do not understand women and cannot really offer any insight, other than this: Unless it is a compliment, you really should not say it. And when in doubt, just *do not say it*. Looking back, there have been many times when what I should have said was nothing. The John Wayne "strong, silent types" remained quiet for good reason.

The main reason I stay married is that I am not sure that I am up to disappointing another woman.

People who study this conclude that money is the source of most stress in relationships. Therefore, the only thing we can suggest for certain is to try to make sure she has some money and a good family, because one always marries the family too. In fact, it might be a case where John McCain got it right when he married a classic beauty queen whose family owns a beer distributorship and is rich. That is what I have called the Southern male's trifecta.

Women have long defied logic to me. Perhaps that is why we men have a hard time pleasing them. For example, I know that women like garage sales and they also like lingerie. But, as I found out the hard way, they do not like lingerie bought at a garage sale.

Every lesson about women we men tend to learn over and over, the hard way. It is just that we are wired differently. Among other oddities, we men can actually leave a hotel room and not make up the bed.

Like cuddling, asking for directions, and listening, we men have to do unnatural things to please a woman. Or we can just become inveterate liars.

Even Bill Clinton has pledged to do all he could to help Hillary get appointed as Secretary of State — even temporarily taking down his eHarmony profile online. See, love can conquer all when it comes to the power of Clinton Inc.

In women's defense, men have always blamed things on them. This has been true since the beginning. When Adam got in trouble with God, he immediately blamed Eve. But the problem we have now with all the equal rights hullabaloo is that women no longer stand for it. This is why we have kids.

When I lament not understanding women, most people quickly suggest books on the subject, mostly written by priests, foreigners, or gay guys who are quick with advice since they really do not have female relationship problems. There was that Mars and Venus book that folks suggested I buy, so I went out and bought it. And now I have the book. Even though I did not read it, when the conversation gets dicey on the male/female subject, I find that if I reference it, all debate stops. The reason, and this is just speculation, is that no one else read it either, and thus mentioning it will end most conversation on the matter.

Some men who are better BS artists tend to survive longer and make women happier than honest men. They only say glowing and positive things, and it is amazing how women keep buying it. They say things like, "My wife and I look at each other today just like we did the first time we saw each other." My initial reaction to this was, "Were you both thinking, 'Wow, I really could do better?'"

As I have aged, I have become smarter about the things I say to women, as they never forget an insult. I know this after a drink was poured on me at a high school reunion by a woman I had not seen in 20 years. I believe it had something to do with my question: "Is that your hair or are you wearing a helmet?"

So I am more careful now. A portly woman who was some 100 pounds overweight told me that she was going to start working out. A few years ago I would have said, "Well, you certainly waited to the last minute." But I have grown as a male (you women would call it evolved) and instead I said, "Oh, come on, you look great and do not need to lose any weight." You see, women are not looking for the truth, so lying is the only way to go. Some call it diplomacy, others self-preservation.

Spring Break:
Life is a Beach

It is the time of the year when a young college man's thoughts turn to romance; and if that does not pan out, he takes a lead from Eliot Spitzer and turns to the Yellow Pages.

We are in the throes of an annual bacchanalian rite in the United States: spring break, wherein our teenaged kids get a crash course in growing up. It is a time when their security deposits, dignity, and virginity get lost, never to be regained.

My Ferris Bueller-like son attends Ole Miss, and he informed me of his plans to take a relaxing week in Destin, Florida for his spring break this year. I wondered out loud to him just what was, if any, the delineation between spring break at Ole Miss and school being in session. He admitted it was merely geographic. I love many things about him, and his honesty when confronted with indisputable facts is one of them.

Well aware of the debauchery that goes on at these spring break trips, I sat my son down and explained the dangers. I told him that messing around with a girl these days could lead to an STD or even worse — a relationship. I told him not to pay for sexual favors unless he had political aspirations to become the New York governor, and that technically, if you pay for it, it is not a favor.

He told me that he felt premarital sex is not a sin if he has no intention of marrying the girl. It was hard to argue with that nuanced logic.

Given the bravado level of the average hormone-saturated young male, I also told my son to be sure that when they went out that at least one of them was sober enough to fight. And if they have known a guy for more than a day, his sister was strictly off limits thereafter. And lastly, I told him that after two drinks, there is a difference between people laughing with you and at you. These were all life lessons I had to learn the hard way.

A lot has changed since my college spring break days. To begin with, we did not have one. But today, as far as I can tell, the *Girls Gone Wild* video library gets expanded on each trip. Also, there have been major advances in beer delivery systems, which primarily involve a rudimentary PVC tube and an owner-operator named "Stoner" barking orders to kids taking bong hits of low-quality beer.

Young men and, hopefully, to a lesser degree women, test their alcohol tolerance on these college trips. Sadly, there is no phase-in period. They go from little or no drinking in high school to *Animal House* the day they hit college.

Most parents worry about kids, mainly because we remember what we were up to at the same age. I know what my son is talking about. While my wild oats have surely turned to bran cereal at this point, and I now only hear my favorite songs on elevators, I do remember what I was like at that age. And that worries me too — a lot. Our kids are usually only as good as the worst one in the group. They tend to gravitate toward him. Sadly, the good kid never brings the others up to his level; he just gets wedgies.

As parents, all we can do is hope that we taught them well how to be responsible. Unlike us, today they have cell phones, so we can check on them. And they are very serious about having a designated driver, unlike their parents. Like many parents, I probably worry about my kids too much. Then I think, oh well, there are always risks in life, and that is what being young is often about. Growing up ain't all it is cracked up to be.

The Upside of All This Downside at Thanksgiving

*"I regard no man as poor who has
a godly mother."*

— Abraham Lincoln

Ever since I was promoted from the children's table to the adult table at age 40 (mostly because I fought with the 12-year-olds), I have valued Thanksgiving dinner. And, I am proud to say that I no longer fight with children, even if they start it.

As my kids begin to scatter to college, we still enjoy each other during this time of year. We do well together as a family — in short doses — as long as there is plenty of booze around and football on TV.

The fact that there are family tensions, liquor, a readily accessible carving knife, and no physical injuries to date at my family's holiday events shows either our love for each other, or a strong respect for the legal system and the rules of evidence with so many witnesses around.

Just to prove that the free-market system is not yet dead, this year the NFL, sensing market demand, will run back-to-back football games on Thanksgiving Day. This will ensure that the males do not have to talk to any relatives they choose not to at any point during the day. We will either be intently watching the game (the Southern Hart males are actually willing to watch the 0 and 11 Detroit Lions just to to avoid family interaction) or eating. In either case, we are not to be talked to.

Thanksgiving is about family, so we all really need to thank our parents first. If your parents never had children, chances are good that you don't either. Depending entirely on which day you ask me, I am proud to say that I have three kids. For some reason we all like to get together on Thanksgiving, mainly because my mother cooks. It is something her generation did, like threshing their own wheat and spending only the money that they had.

The bad news is that I eat too much, but the good news is that I do not exercise either. One does not get this out of shape by accident. I actually am in shape, but that shape is a pear. I did join a gym once, but later found out that I actually had to go to it and work out to stay in shape. I hate when they mislead people into joining gyms like that. So I no longer work out.

Well, that is not entirely true; I do work out on occasion. Every now and then I will be in the bathtub, pull the plug, and just fight the current. I think the President's Council on Physical Fitness rates that right up there with riding an escalator.

Comforted by the fact that the Heimlich maneuver has been perfected, each year I gorge myself with a 20,000-calorie Thanksgiving dinner that would feed an African village for a week. It is why six of ten Americans are overweight — the other four are illegal immigrants.

In fact, if you want to know why the world hates us, we have a TV game show called *Survivor,* where Americans can win one million dollars by just living in another country for a week. How do you think those folks who live in that country feel when the film crews leave? Wow! Americans will pay one of their folks to live here for just a week and "survive."

We did not become the most hated country in the world by just bombing other countries and imposing our will. If we have learned anything from the French, it is that to be really disliked we have to muster up some arrogance too.

I truthfully think we are the best country on the planet, and I regard the media-conjured hate of us by the rest of the world as what it is: envy. Our poor live better than the upper class in most countries — for now. And with the stock market down 50% and the coming "redistribution" of what wealth is left, our rich live just like the poor.

A friend told me the stock market being down is worse than a divorce. You lose half your money and you still have to be married.

The upside of all of this downside in the economy is that we all might appreciate family and friends more around this time of year. Having confused wants with needs and the American dream with rights, we are all over-extended in the material world. Being a bit poorer this season may make us appreciate the simpler pleasures of life. And maybe we will eat less.

Christmas in the Guilted Age

We finally did in the Hart family what I have secretly wanted to do for years: we agreed not to exchange Christmas presents. Sadly, we decided this a bit late as I took off December 9th to shop, unknowingly on "Call In to Work Gay Day," which, along with my stylish new tighter-fitting pants, has done nothing to quell the office rumors about me.

While it took some family members time to get their heads around the idea, not giving gifts this year has worked remarkably well. Those in the family who opposed it when we sent out e-mails telling them that we were not going to get into the one-upmanship of present buying this year have now really embraced the idea.

We suggested donating to charity, helping a needy local family, volunteering, or perhaps pooling our Christmas money and bidding for Barack Obama's U.S. Senate in Illinois that Governor Blagojevich has for sale. In the past there have been lesser suggestions that I did not like, like the year

we said no booze and no watching football so we could spend quality time talking to the family — I referred to that as the "lose-lose scenario."

The idea that Christmas has become a pressure-packed ritual of buying for our family in return for them buying for us in equal measure misses the intent. When did bringing frankincense and myrrh morph into buying Xboxes and Wii for bratty kids?

The excesses in America have gotten so bad that my family, unbeknownst to me, even bought a sweater for our cat. A sweater for a cat! Or, as the cat concluded when we gave it to him, not food. No wonder the world hates us.

My buddies are the same way about this time of year, so we all leave the house full of relatives and join each other at what we call the "Buckhead Ballet" in Atlanta for the annual Nativity Scene and some North Pole dancing. In fact, in this economy many women who used to have high powered jobs in corporate America find it more lucrative to work at strip clubs. Instead of climbing the corporate ladder they are now sliding down the brass pole. We like to support the local artists and are quick to do so at this time of year. We don't express it, because we are men, but we all feel cooped up and pressured by "The Season" and need to get away. Loaded up with guilt and booze makes it easier to endure the holidays.

So many families have more than they need. Want is often disguised as need. And if we want something, we tend to get it for ourselves.

The awkward annual ritual of having to strategize and anticipate what family members and friends want for Christmas is a no-win proposition. Then we get in our SUVs and head to crowded malls (which historically do not have sales before Christmas) to buy Chinese-made trinkets or poorly fitting clothes for family.

Personally, I like crowded malls about as much as Paris Hilton enjoys *Jeopardy*. I think the reason I do not like crowds is that I really do not like people, and crowds invariably involve lots of people. This, according to my favorite source, *Gross Generalities* magazine.

Then comes the ritual of the giving of the gift.

The only thing acted out in America more around this time of year than a Charles Dickens play is the "just what I wanted" face that 90 percent of us feign. The pressure of having to like a present may be worse than the self-induced pressure to please someone with a gift. I find both unnecessarily stressful in equal measure.

Partially to blame is the advertising of Madison Avenue. Ironically, the liberals in New York say they oppose everything capitalistic, yet they make commercials implying that you are a jerk if you do not hand your mate keys to a Lexus sitting in the driveway with a bow on it. If you want to give your spouse a car, that is fine with me, especially since O.J. Simpson will be making the license plate. But being guilted into buying by overly suggestive ads is not good, and it leaves most of us feeling inadequate.

Perhaps this explains Americans' problem with debt.

I have always found it hypocritical the way the New York Times will have a maudlin article about, say, starvation in Darfur juxtaposed with a Saks Fifth Avenue ad for a $1,250 pair of Gucci shoes.

It seems ironic that the two men most admired by the liberals at the New York Times are Hugo Chavez and Hugo Boss. Too many folks will buy that $1,250 pair of shoes to wear to a $100 fundraiser that is way more social than charitable.

Men are particularly hard hit this time of year. Since we clearly have no idea what women want the other 364 days of the year, it is unrealistic to expect that we will guess right on Christmas. Men have wasted more time doing this than video buffering.

In the vein of "What would Jesus do?" I think we all need to evaluate what Christmas really is and we have allowed it to become. Christmas seems to have evolved into something more like "What would Donald Trump do?"

Perhaps we are too willing to live for the here and now and to go into debt for things we do not need. We must take care of those who we know need the basics of life first.

If Hurricane Katrina taught us anything, it is that our dysfunctional government cannot take care of the citizens of this country. The only hope that government will protect us from another ice age is that glaciers are moving from the Arctic toward us at an inch a year. Government should be able to formulate a plan by the year 2992.

Those who can afford a $400 video game that our kids will toss aside before the last football bowl game is over should consider how good it would be to give that money to an efficient soup kitchen in their area. That is truly the spirit of Christmas.

Keeping Up With Old Friends

"A friend is, as it were, a second self."

— Cicero, Roman author, orator and politician

After attending the championship game of the NCAA Final Four and being devastated by the result — my alma mater lost in overtime — I hosted some old friends at my home in Florida. We planned to watch the Masters and celebrate the 25th year of our friendship, which began in the training program at Goldman Sachs. Friends came from as far away as London to catch up, reminisce, and compare life's lessons, but mostly they came for the golf and a free shot at my liquor cabinet.

We are all sniffing 50 now and are starting to make sounds like coffee makers. Of all the things that we wanted to be as we got older, pear-shaped and shiny were not two of them. We looked like we were filming a Flomax commercial.

If you have not had that poignant moment when you are sitting at dinner with old friends and you start to share reading glasses, then I hope that someday that you will. And I hope you will smile about it the way we did last week.

It is truly amazing — the success of our twenty-five young MBA grads of the Goldman class of 1983. None of the hires came from money. All set upon a quest to build something for themselves from scratch. Contrary to what you are told by the populist media, Wall Street does not look for rich, preppy, and connected kids. They do not want to work too hard on you in that business. As a result, Wall Street is one of the best ways out for those of us with limited means growing up. Wall Street wants the hungry, smart, and creative ones with the energy and confidence to make things happen. They often like the athletes or military school grads who understand teamwork and how to compete.

As hard as it is for the PC crowd to accept, historically successful hires are the "guy's guy" types. Rarely does someone who starts in corporate America whining about how the company should do more about global warming or Tibet end up being worth much financially. J.B. Fuqua once said that the business of business *is* business. Correcting perceived societal wrongs and slights is not the goal of business.

If you hire someone who frets about that or who has a hyphenated name, you might as well hire an attorney to defend the inevitable lawsuit. They have a place for these folks, easily identified by e-mail addresses that end in .org, .gov or .edu. Not business, where only the quantifiably tough survive. It is non-racist and the ultimate in fair.

After leaving the firm in pursuit of entrepreneurial endeavors, some in the group built nice companies, employed people, and paid more than their share of taxes. And in a country that boos the winners, most find it more sensible to downplay their success (those that do not believe in this are named Trump) for fear of resentment or envy. We found comfort in sharing successes with those who could appreciate them the most. As John McEnroe said, "Everybody loves success, but they hate successful people."

Often the hardest thing about success is finding someone who is genuinely happy for you. It was clear that everyone there with us this week was profoundly proud of each other.

The confidence to take such business risks, and the ability to make a vision a reality, can be traced in some measure to our becoming friends at that young age, in that time and place called Goldman Sachs. The guts to become an entrepreneur can be gained from seeing friends do it and with their encouragement.

Most in my crowd of the class of 1983 are now in pursuit of things that cannot be bought. Most have started foundations. Some, although late to their kids' lives, are focusing on them now. And in the world they have created that is different from their childhoods, they are facing the challenges of raising appreciative and grounded kids. A few are testing their capacity for the enjoyment of wealth, which, contrary to popular wisdom, is not a given for a driven person. Money does not come with instructions.

If there is one thing that we all agree on after 25 years of marriage and having daughters, it is that we do not understand women.

We long since stopped trying to figure out why we men do what we do. At some age you just accept and celebrate the differences.

It seems abundantly clear that the ability to nurture and maintain friendships is crucial to a person's success in life. Any difficulties in business, family, politics, sports, and the like can be made bearable with the advice and support of a like-minded friend who knows you. Baron Rothschild listed as one of his axioms: "Make no useless friends." In life, you only have time for a few. Make them count.

Old friends will always be the best ones, so you have to keep them around if for no other reason than the fact that they know too much about you.

(l-r) Barry Hines, Ron Hart, Scott Lucas and Tom Albertson in 1983.

(l-r) Top row: Scott Lucas, Mark Fife, Tom Albertson, Ron; bottom row: Rick Elman, Barry Hines and Peter Mallinson

A Place in Our Hearts
For SEC Football

"We are inclined to think that if we watch a
football game, we have taken part in it."

— John F. Kennedy

As a Southerner I know and appreciate Southeastern Conference football; much in the same way a Northerner appreciates say, a snow blower or a corrupt big-city mayor. And, since I did not attend an SEC school, I can be objective in writing on the matter.

My football career was unremarkable at best, but the crowd always cheered for me. I'd like to think they liked me, but I really think it was more like folks cheering for a Special Olympian or when George Bush finishes a long sentence. Either way, it was nice, and my dad was proud.

One such experience was as a back-up quarterback in a game that we were losing by 30 points with three minutes left. All of a sudden the crowd in the stands started yelling, "We want Ron, we want Ron, we want Ron." I looked to see if my dad was still in the stands, but sadly he had left early to get his car, as traffic was notoriously bad leaving a small town's football game, with a record of 2 and 8.

However, the crowd's chant of "We want Ron" got the attention of the head coach and he motioned me over. Excited about some playing time, I put my helmet on and ran to him. Coach looked at me and said, "Ron, go see what those folks want."

With my experience and those of countless other boys in the South, we all appreciate football. It is something that we can enjoy watching with our family — without having to actually talk to them.

SEC football holds a special place in our hearts because of its pure roots and rabid Southern fan base. While it is not as pure as it once was, given the corruption of money and NCAA rules that are more convoluted than Michael Jackson's sexual orientation, it still appeals to all of us at some instinctive level — just above cock-fighting, but not quite as much as some of those Jerry Springer episodes you can only buy on tape. In fact, one of the proudest moments for my family was when my sister got to sing the National Anthem at a cock fight.

Barry Switzer, the legendary coach of the University of Oklahoma, took a job coaching the Dallas Cowboys. When asked how college football differed from professional football he said, "Well, in college football, we had no salary cap."

Therein lies the problem — one I addressed in a column about Mike Price's troubles at the University of Alabama entitled, "Win one for the Stripper" years ago. It seems Coach Price got fired because he donated money to charity.

Sadly, in this case Charity was purportedly a topless dancer in Pensacola. But, in that column, which was Pulitzer-Prize eligible, brilliant, witty, and hours ahead of its time, I said that the NCAA ought to pay players of big money Division 1 schools some money for their efforts and end the hypocrisy.

So why not go ahead and recognize college football for what it is, simply a farm system for the NFL? There is no shame in that. English majors are just a farm system for unemployed writers who now blog on liberal websites.

Everyone goes to college to train for a job; that is what these guys are doing. Pretending that a kid is at Nebraska to study biology may be what the NCAA says in its ads, but we know it is not true.

I was once asked, "Do you know what the 'N' on the Nebraska helmet stands for?" The answer: Knowledge. (This joke works better when delivered aloud.)

Few, if any, of these kids would be in college if it were not for football. Therefore, they are simply occupying a spot that a student who really wants to study biology should have. In other words, an Asian kid. Ironically, the most liberal and prestigious academic colleges are the ones that stretch the most to get a kid in who plays football or basketball.

They call it their "diversity" efforts. So it goes a bit like this: you are diverse if you play football at Harvard and have a 900 SAT score, and you are not diverse if you grow up white in a trailer park, are a lead singer of a country band with a 900 SAT, and are denied admission.

Lastly, and while I am on this Andy Rooney-like rant, why not have two distinct divisions in college football? One for the big BCS contenders (I think BCS stands for Biased California System), and another one for traditionally pure student athletes programs like the one at Vanderbilt, Rice, Duke, or Tulane. Perhaps a Kudzu League for the better academic schools in the South?

And why is it that major college programs, like the University of Georgia, cannot kick Murray State and Louisiana Tech off their schedules and allow for a year-ending playoff to decide the national title instead of the BCS rankings? How can a bunch of BCS sports writers compare University of Southern California to a team like Auburn if they don't play each other? Most sportswriters can't compare their plaid jacket to their striped pants — much less an SEC team to a PAC 10 one.

I do love watching an SEC football game with my dad. And, at some point toward the end of his life, I plan to tell him I love him. But then I fear I might misjudge the timing as we have longevity in our family and he might live ten more years, and that would just be too awkward for both of us.

So, like most guys, it is just easier to watch SEC football with him — for now.

Life Lessons From Coach Cartwright

"A winner must first know what losing is like."

— Malcolm Forbes

One of the greats in Columbia, Tennessee history is being honored on May 14 with a roast that I am hosting to raise money for a new indoor practice facility. That man, who influenced the lives of thousands of young men during his thirty-year career as head football coach at Columbia Central High School, is Jim Cartwright.

When I was a student there, his record was slightly better than the Washington Generals, (the Harlem Globe Trotters' perennial opponents), yet he profoundly influenced the lives of many young men in Columbia for two generations.

I have been reminded of Coach Cartwright many times in the past thirty years. Watching the movie *Remember the Titans* reminded me of how football bridged the race gap in the 1970s in many towns torn by integration. The movie was just like Central High School; the only differences were was that the Titans actually won and the actors were good-looking.

There has probably never been a better arena for black and white kids to get to know and trust each other than football. Football was color-blind, fair, and brought character to light like no other sport. And it was life for many kids. The friendships young men forge at such an impressionable age can last a lifetime.

A good man like Coach Cartwright meant a lot to boys like us, some of whom had no father at home, no discipline in their lives, or no place to go after school.

And, as I sensed at the time, football was going to be the pinnacle of some of these kids' lives. To this day, it is what we talk about when we get together and was probably more important than anything we learned in school. I broke my hip and stayed on the team as a trainer, as I had grown close to my teammates. I was so slow that I could barely rustle leaves, cowardly by nature, and was about 140 pounds of asthma, so it was no great loss to the team. Staying around the team was important to me, however, and it molded my thinking of boys developing into men and how important a role a coach or mentor plays.

Coach Cartwright was never a holier-than-thou guy. He was a guy's guy, the type of rough-and-tumble guy that other guys like. I have seen it in business and life since then; it is the guy that is the likable scoundrel to whom the other guys are drawn. These are guys you play golf with, and the guys you would want beside you in a war or in a bar fight. And for those around football, we all remember the sights, the sounds, and the smells. Especially the locker room smell — now *that* stays with you.

The only bowl game that I remember aspiring to was the Tobacco Bowl, which, if I remember CHS in 1977 correctly, probably involved the players and all the coaches actually using tobacco during the game.

I remember how Coach Cartwright would throw his visor on the ground to protest a referee's call, which seemed to always go against us. You could always tell he was mad as he ever could be when he threw his visor on the ground and stomped on it ... almost as mad as he was in the previous quarter of the game when he had last done it! And I remember his nose. Lord, what a nose. It was so big and had been broken so many times it made you feel like you had been hit in the nose. His face looked like a Picasso.

When I first met him, he wore those big black-rimmed glasses like they issued to Vietnam soldiers. When he took them off the first time, I swear I thought his nose and eyebrows were going to come with them. And I do remember the three-a-day football camps and the hazing of players. The discipline was important because boys, as a gender, we really ain't much until we are about 25. And even then, we are only as good as we were raised. Contrary to what teachers' unions or Child Services tell you, the possibility of bodily harm was often the only thing that made us pay attention.

Simply asking us to do something for the twenty-fifth time really does not work, nor does logic or coddling. They used to haze and toughen up a boy with various rites of passage. Now everyone is so PC and scared to discipline kids that they have gone soft, bratty, and ready to sue at the slightest imposition of discipline. And that is too bad.

We give away ninth-place ribbons and coddle, stroke, and coax kids to a point that their expectations are so out of line that they cannot function. And, honestly, teachers telling all the kids that they can grow up to be astronauts is just cruel. Who are they kidding? With all the shallow complimenting we give boys today, the only job they are suited for is to be Liza Minnelli's next husband.

What we learned from Coach Cartwright was that if he liked you, he made fun of you. And if he did not like you, he did not make fun of you. He taught us to be men and to value our team more than ourselves. And although we did not win, playing football was about the camaraderie and life experience more than anything else.

For all the lifelong friendships forged under the watchful one good eye of Coach Cartwright, we are all eternally grateful.

Coach Cartwright died April 5, 2008 at the age of 74.

Peyton's Place in History

*"The best teachers of humanity
are the lives of great men."*

— Charles Flowers, author

I hope you watched Super Bowl 41, or XLI M.C. HAMMEREMC2XMCC for those less numerically inclined Romans still out there. Prince performed, in what proved to be a perfectly symbolically linear event, as he, too, is represented by a symbol (♀). This helps to further reinforce the notion that Prince is just a regular guy like you and me.

The Super Bowl is like the Tony Awards for us heterosexual guys. Apparently the rest of the country was watching, too, as this Super Bowl was the third most-watched show in history. Even with no promise of a wardrobe malfunction, and in the purple rain, America tuned in to see Peyton win.

Now I do not like to talk about it, but Peyton and I are friends. We began playing golf at a club in Tennessee five years ago. Because I work during the week and he works weekends, I do not see him much in the fall and winter. But when the season is over, we hit the links, and spend time at each other's second homes. And just to confirm, he is the greatest.

Watching him call signals last Sunday, it may have seemed like he was trying to auction off some farm equipment, land a jet, or order an overly elaborate Subway sandwich. But you can rest assured; there is no one who understands football and life better than Peyton.

Having to endure the constant second-guessing of potbellied sports writers, most of whom did not start for their high school JV teams, he proved what we all knew: He does have the right stuff, and he can win the big one. After spotting the Bears a touchdown on the opening kickoff, the Colts won the game with ease. It looked like the Bears, along with the rest of America, wanted Peyton to help cement his legacy.

With his place in history now firmly established, he can focus on his real dream: perfecting his alternative interpretive tango dance moves, starring in a Broadway musical, or becoming a scratch golfer. I can't remember which. Alternatively, now that he has won the Super Bowl, he will catch the eye of the Canadian Football League and get an offer from them. I am told there are provinces way up there in northern Canada that have never seen him in a commercial.

Even with his winning, the race-obsessed media could not help but wear out the fact that two African-American head coaches were in the Super Bowl. In reality, it is only in the media's mind that race gets inserted into every event. Most of America really has moved past all that. It probably would not even been an issue if it had not been brought up by every commentator ad nauseam. If a coach can win, he will coach. There is nothing more colorblind than the desire to win, or true free market capitalism. The best person is put in the best position by those seeking a desired outcome — winning.

Even in the 1970s, if an NFL team owner thought Jimmie "J.J. Dyn-o-mite" Walker would win them a Super bowl as coach, he would have been hired. At some point, the media needs to focus on people's ability, not always on their race. Tiger Woods agrees.

Now maybe I am rare, as I do not see race. I know I am white because people tell me I am very white, a lot. And it must be true, as I never get followed around by security in malls and I once drove a week with a tail light out and did not get beat up by the police. I jokingly said in a speech recently to test the humor of the crowd that we should not discriminate based on race. If a person acts white, that should be good enough. But at some point, we just need to let all this go and just make fun of people without it always being called racist. We have free speech in this country — as long, of course, as it is not about race or Israel.

Getting back to Peyton and his future, here is my guess. He finishes out with the Colts, then backs up for a few years with the Titans all the while mentoring a young quarterback. Then he coaches and later runs for the U.S. Senate as a Republican from Tennessee. How is that for going out on a limb? I just hope this does not make it into a newspaper or a book or something, where I will be held accountable for this prediction in the future.

Peyton Manning and Ron Hart

Why Daddy Drinks

No Such Thing As A *Pretty Good* Alligator Wrestler

*"The desire not to be anything
is the desire not to be."*

— Ayn Rand

Recently I stayed home from work for a day. It was my first sick day in five years and, hopefully, the last. If my male pride does not keep me working until I am ninety-nine years old, the thought of having to watch daytime television will.

Like most of you, I prefer to live my miserable life vicariously through shallow, albeit better looking, people. We know them as celebrities. They are all over daytime TV. Just so you do not have to do this, here is a summary of what happened last week while you were working, like most people, to advance our GNP or raise our kids.

Brad Pitt and Angelina Jolie had their baby and named her "Shiloh" as they felt being their kid would not call enough attention to her. This was Angelina's third child but her first with a man. They thought about naming her "Antietam" or "Appomattox." I would suggest "Bull Run," but they felt "Shiloh" was right. I think it was an Indian name which, loosely translated, means "idiot parents."

Apparently Rosie O'Donnell took Meredith Vieira's place on *The View*, a daytime women's talk show that is more like a full hour of screaming. The scandal is that Rosie and fellow heavyweight Star Jones do not get along. Given all this, I just do not think I can watch *The View* anymore. Not because I don't like four women cackling about their feelings all day, but because I would just feel so sorry for that couch. As a parting shot to them, I would suggest that with Rosie now on the show, and in the spirit of full disclosure, they should change the name to *The Obstructed View*. Rosie O'Donnell's joining *The View* is bad news for the New York Dragons arena football team that she will now have to quit.

The good news is that with all the cable channels available, you can watch The History Channel or the Discovery Channel during the day. I thought about watching a show on the Ottoman Empire. I just think it is a great idea to have your society based on having your feet comfortable while sitting. I found out they were warmongers, so I just turned to CNN to see how we were doing in Iraq.

I also watched that Australian guy, "the Croc Hunter," who screams at the TV as he idiotically tries to find and start a fight with alligators. It seems like a dangerous job, almost like being on *The View*. I heard this guy was "a great alligator wrestler." But then it dawned on me, there is no such thing as a "pretty good alligator wrestler." It is akin to being a 60-year-old Kamikaze pilot; it just does not ring true.

I also saw Tom Cruise appear a show in an attempt to convince women that he is not weird. He is supposed to be promoting his latest installment of *Mission Impossible 12* or something, which I think involves him trying to find out who got his wife, Katie Holmes, pregnant. Then Maureen Dowd came on to promote her book *Are Men Necessary?*, which I can only speculate is about her inability to get a date.

Between the soaps, the women's shows, which are over 50 percent commercials (most seem to be advertising some form of hygiene product that I am afraid they will tell me exactly what it is for), and the plaintiffs' lawyer commercials (no doubt preying on the lazy butts at home looking for a way out of working again), daytime at home is no place for most people. It became clear to me that I would rather work until I die than to stay home and watch daytime TV. If that will not get a man back to work pronto, nothing will.

Now I know that when these high-powered CEOs say they are going to resign to spend more time with their families, they are full of it. My suggestion to them is when you say that "you are going to spend more time with your family," you ought to check with the family first. You might get an opposing opinion from them.

Your wife married you for "better or worse," not for lunch. Marriages work as long as you both have a lot of time and space — space being the most important of these. And, that dream of doing some "wood-working out in your garage" ain't so appealing come day three.

My guess is that most baby-boomers will work longer for money, health (staying active keeps your mind sharp), social connections, and the most recent reason I discovered — to avoid daytime TV.

Summertime, and the Olympics are Sleazy

As a typical Southern male, I have never been a big fan of the Winter Olympics. Men's figure skating — you know it as ice dancing — and two-man luge just do not seem right to me. They smack of a personal matter between two consenting adults, not sport.

I also question the honesty of the Olympics and think at least one male ice skater has tested positive for heterosexuality. My suspicion rose about him when I found out that he did not actually sew his own ice-dancing outfit.

My hope is that, if global warming is not the crock (a la Y2K) that I think it is, the upside might be the end of the Winter Olympics.

For the United States to even compete in the Winter Olympics is silly. We should never attempt an international sporting event where we put ourselves in a position to actually lose to Norway — at anything.

Mexico, for example, falls into this category. I am actually surprised they can field a team since every able-bodied person with reasonable foot speed is now in the United States. One notable fact about the Mexican fencing team: they actually build fences.

Naturally, it is hard for France to field a team as every time the starting pistol goes off, their team, by force of habit, surrenders.

I thought I was not a big fan of the Summer Olympics either, the ones with gymnastics, track, and archery. Historically, the Olympic Games combine two things that I do not like: P.E. class and foreigners. Yet by day fifteen of my refusal to watch the Olympics, I had not missed a single night's broadcast.

Just to summarize, I did like women's beach volleyball. I cannot put my finger on it, but I found that "sport" compelling. For the first time, I felt good about the money I spent on my high-definition TV. As for women's water polo, somehow it does not have the same appeal. All that neck-high water seems to defeat the purpose and might discourage a strong male viewership. I would suggest putting a shark in the pool; then you'd have something. Perhaps I should pitch such a show to NBC for the fall reality show line-up.

My kids discovered what we adults are reminded of every four years: Bob Costas really is a smart guy and is just a bit taller than a Chinese "woman" gymnast. We also are reminded (by the mainstream media) that, even though the world hates America, all the athletes who are able come here to train and live. This seems an interesting contradiction.

And for the Chinese, there was excitement in the air about the Olympics. There were also dioxin, lead, chloride, and mercury. The air in Beijing is thicker than the smoke in Snoop Dogg's limo on a Saturday night. Three archery contestants shot their arrow in that event and they got stuck in the smog.

As expected, Michael Phelps was the American hero in these games. He represented us Americans well by eating 12,000 calories a day while the world watched. Polls indicate that other countries hate America most because of our gluttony. I think Ryan Seacrest was listed as a close second.

China won so many medals that they will probably melt them down and sell them back to Americans in items to be sold at Dollar Tree stores. Then there was a kid from Alabama who won a gold medal and was so proud of it that he said he was going to have it bronzed. All heart-warming stories of human triumph.

You can't have the Olympics without human rights protesters. Many wanted to know about the way China treats Tibet, but that was confined to Hollywood actors who really do not know enough to have a follow-up question on the matter.

The U.S. did open itself up to the same question about human rights violations to Gitmo detainees, but Vice-President Cheney deflected the question on the matter by saying it was not torture, just yoga with a CIA instructor. So that should put all of that to rest.

For all its attributes, China just does not want to play nice with other countries in the sand box. Understandably, that is a problem for China because none of its people have grown up with sibling rivalry. They want things their way, so much so that they proved to us that they do not card their women gymnasts. There is no minimum age in China to compete in the Olympics or to work in a factory, which is where discarded gymnasts end up once they are tall enough to reach the sewing machines.

China did give condoms out to all male American athletes when they arrived, and I am sure they gave extras to our men's basketball team, which is composed of NBA players. In fact, there are few things in more conflict than Communist China's Draconian one-child policy and the personal conduct of our NBA players. They probably did not let the players make eye contact with their women.

In the past, the Olympics were more of a test of which country had the best pharmacists and geneticists. If you liked amazing performances followed by tearful apologies, then the Olympics were for you. This year they got the testing right. They even had tests for testosterone levels to make sure some of the women were not actually men. If this test is effective, Janet Reno and Rosie O'Donnell will be tested soon.

As a former man who became a woman, Renee Richards should discuss this. Her/his tennis career, which started at Yale, was cut short when he/she could not pass the Olympics chromosome test. I remember reading about it in his/her autobiography, which I believe was called *How to Play Tennis Without Balls*.

Overall, the Olympics benefit us by exhibiting how other countries go about their business. We saw how Communist China's government intervenes to organize and control all that its citizens do. It is good for us to see this, as it will give us a glimpse of what Barack Obama and Nanny Pelosi have in store for America when elected.

Everybody Loves a Random Ass-Whooping

Recently I was driving to God's Country — Tennessee — and got a call from the office on my cell. This always troubles me, because when I leave the office I leave specific instructions, "If anyone needs me, I will call them."

My assistant gave me a few messages and awkwardly said, "Did you hear the news around the office?"

I said, "No, have they finally gotten around to auditing the Travel and Expense reports and decided to fire me?" "No," she said, and went into an interesting scenario unfolding that had our office of some eighty people speculating all day.

A man had called the receptionist and said that there was a guy in our office having an affair with his wife, and that he was "coming up there at 4:00 pm to whoop his ass." This Roy D. Mercer-style fight had captivated the imagination of the office. He left this message with a man who, after just twenty-four years in the business, had been catapulted to receptionist. Ever the linear thinker, he wrote the message down — verbatim.

Then our ever self-protecting management awoke. Startled from their nap, they sprung into action by calling security. "Security," in our building, entails a guy in an ill-fitting blazer who leans on his desk and hollers at all the women in the lobby, asking them "Whazzz up?"

Of the forty-five or so men in the office, forty of them were real nervous for the next hour or so. The other five were online looking at fabric or planning a cruise with their life partners.

Thirty of the forty men left the office abruptly to attend an unscheduled "appointment." Then the enraged husband called back, oddly enough, to ask for directions. Our receptionist told him how to get there and reminded him to bring up his parking ticket, as we validate.

The receptionist did have the presence of mind to ask him his name and who may he say should expect an ass whooping by 4:00? "My name is Chad," he said, and he thought the philanderers name was Greg, but he was working on the specifics. Word quickly spread. The two Gregs in our office were already "gone for the day."

Now there is nothing we Americans love more than a pending ass whoopin' of someone other than ourselves. It reminded me of the Roy D. Mercer recordings that I so love, yet with an with an urban twist. The only thing that could make this better would be if he said he was bringing his brother. And there are a lot of guys at my office that could use a severe and comprehensive ass whooping, so this thing was really panning out great for me.

I suggested to "management" that we put a trainee in the lobby and tell him it was "role play day" and that his name was to be Greg. Management liked the idea, but felt it left them open to litigation. "Fine," I said. "Don't expect to get any more great ideas from me if you trample them." I provide little to the office except laughter, which is indeed "the best medicine." And, since they are provided no prescription drug plan, employees view that as valuable.

I got to Nashville and it was 4:15 Eastern Time so I called the office to see what happened. Sadly, the guy had not shown. He said he would be there by 4:00 and was not there. I remarked that it is just rude not to call if you are running late.

The day ended with no whoopin', but my staff stayed past 5:00 for the first time with me out of town in probably, well, ever.

The next day we found out that this guy's wife just made up someone's name to hack off her jealous husband, probably to throw him off the scent of the real boyfriend. It was, however, quite a study in human nature at our otherwise staid office. Like everyone, I am just redneck enough to want to see some action. We all love train wrecks, which is why we watch

Jerry Springer, Courtney Love, and Gary Busey on TV, or "Hooked on Phonics" George Bush giving an unscripted press conference.

Maybe anthropologists can explain why we all love an all-out fight. I love watching those Ultimate Fighters named "Butterbean", "The Magic Hispanic", or "The Irish Hand Grenade" who fight on those cable channels way up in the 180s. Now those guys are really fighting for something; probably the next title loan payment on their pawned car.

I personally have started many fights in my life, but at 165 pounds of asthma, always declined to participate in them. But this story does remind us, as did Hurricane Katrina, just how primitive we all are. Bubbling very near the surface of even the most white-collar executives is the innate desire to see someone, other than themselves, get beat up.

Goodbye Mr. Chaps

I am starting to feel like Forrest Gump, an easily bemused spectator who happens by chance upon all kinds of interesting events.

This time I was in New York City moving one of my children home from New York University when, in an attempt to meet an old friend for lunch, I ran into the Gay Pride Parade. I would say backed into it, but that could be wrongly interpreted.

It was an unfortunate time for me to be visiting New York City. With all the Gay Priding going on in New York that day, it was a difficult time to get your hair done, see a Broadway musical, or get a good waiter.

For those of you who do not have a Gay Pride Parade in your town, here is what I make of it: the overall message of the parade is a bit unclear, but from what I could discern with absolute certainty, they like to express themselves through dance.

In one word, the parade was fabulous! As you might imagine, it was pretty decadent, with drag queens and lesbohemians a-plenty. Let's just say that Norman Rockwell would not choose to paint this slice of Americana.

My long-documented philosophy on gays simply says that when our government runs billion dollar deficits, and cannot find 12 million illegal aliens or Osama bin Laden, balance the budget, or wage useful wars, then it should really not spend too much time trying to tell consenting people what to do in private.

Like most men, I am not a fan of the mechanics of gay guy sex, or feminine hygiene issues, but I know that it is not my business and really try not to think about it. Conversely, on the lesbian side, I follow a comfortable double standard. Most of us men really like to believe that any good looking woman is just two Jagermeister shooters away from some girl-on-girl action.

Michael Bloomberg, the recently outed independent, no longer Republican-in-the-closet mayor of New York, led the parade. Hardcore Republicans believe that being gay is a choice. Bloomberg, like an increasing number of us Americans, knows that being a Republican is also a choice.

I have said that Libertarians have about as much power in the GOP as Log Cabin Republicans, but their Halloween parties are not near as much fun.

The most surprising thing for me was the large numbers of churches that sponsored floats. I counted no fewer than forty gay church groups marching in the parade. Some held signs like Dykes for Christ and Dyke Deacons. There were even Baptists, but the Episcopalians had the edge. The marchers for one venerable New Jersey church had a great sign that said; "Our church is 100 years old, but our thinking is not."

Senator Chuck Schumer, D-N.Y., was there, but noticeably absent was the "odds on favorite" of actually being a lesbian, Hillary Clinton — the other white meat senator from New York. She is busy recasting herself as a centrist for the upcoming election, and you really don't do that by participating in things that you really believe in.

The gay pride marchers obviously have a lot in common, even beyond that fact that they all have at least one framed picture of a pet in their apartment. They are in this quest to be liked or at least accepted by people who, for some religion-driven reason, hate them. But to parade around in front of kids wearing just a G-string, throwing condoms to the crowd is probably not the best way to achieve likeability and acceptance.

In addition, we must realize that much of what the gay rights movement is pushing for is symbolic. Reportedly, the first lesbian couple to marry under the Massachusetts law that first allowed it divorced shortly thereafter. I wonder who got to keep the flannel shirts and who got the Indigo Girls CD's?

I truly believe that gay people are born that way. It is not a choice. If you saw some of these parade participants, you would agree that they are eaten up with the gay gene. They did not "catch gay" one day. God made them that way. It is, however, a choice to do decadent things in public in order to provoke a reaction.

It does not help their cause when they push too many things in our faces. *Will and Grace* and the many hairdressers and interior decorators who have improved our appearance do more to advance the acceptance of gays than the in-your-face, Rosie O'Donnell style of confrontation.

As a casual observer, I could not tell if the parade was a protest or a party; neither could the participants. As times change, they really need to rethink their message. Even *The New York Observer,* in a column cleverly entitled "Goodbye, Mr. Chaps," agreed. It said many prominent gay leaders shun the 37-year-old parade as no longer trendy or needed. And if gays are anything, they are fashionable.

Lap Dance of Luxury:
Strippers Teach Econ 101

Cost of undergraduate degree from Georgia Tech: $100,000
Night of partying at a strip club: $53,000
Dad's reaction to son's $53,000 one-night bill: priceless

It has happened again! A Florida man says that his son was taken advantage of by a Panhandle strip joint. The father gave his son his credit card to celebrate his graduation from Georgia Tech and the boy ran up a $53,000 tab. It appears that the strippers were the only ones who got a happy ending.

I guess the son, catapulted to an undergrad degree at age twenty-four, didn't learn the economics of real life. Chief among them is to never give strippers a free shot at your credit card when you are drunk.

Much like their brethren, lawyers, strippers quickly size up potential clients for what they can fleece from them based on how much money they have and how naïve they appear.

I have always supported the honest entrepreneur, especially when pitted against the stupid. It is good for society when money is not left too long in idiot hands. It is God's way of getting money into smarter folks' pockets. For the less religious among us, I call it Economic Darwinism, and it is often done one crumpled $5 bill at a time. As the old saying goes, "A fool and his money are soon parted." In this case, a fool and his dad's money were soon partying.

I do not understand these men who spend silly amounts of money in strip clubs. I have had friends whose longest female relationships have lasted just two table dances. Men go to these clubs to make themselves feel important because somewhere in their life they are lacking in self-esteem or affirmation. They are paying for the illusion of being a big shot and are suspended briefly in the thought that these women actually think they are attractive. They often get buyer's remorse when the stripper's cooing and ego-stroking ends, which invariably happens right when the guy's money runs out. Who knew?

Surprisingly, our government, which likes to wet its beak in all vices, has yet to devise a way to muscle in on the strip joint business. But it will someday. The feds paid farmers to grow tobacco, taxed cigarettes, and then pushed lawsuits against cigarette manufacturers. Governments are now into gambling, sponsoring their own state lotteries (akin to running numbers). They license casinos, mostly for Native Americans, to relieve their guilt so Indians can get Manhattan back — one nickel slot at a time. And of course, there is booze, where government takes an inordinate cut of the sales of alcohol. Then there was the Mustang Ranch bordello that the Feds once took over and tried to run. Only our government could be as inept as to not make money selling sex and booze. They later sold it.

For the youngsters out there, it is best to view the government as a mob boss, without the protection or moral consistency. Government's involvement in all things vice related is how it establishes the moral high ground that allows it to tax us and tell us how we should conduct our lives.

I do not go to strip clubs. It is not that I have any opposition to them. Your average stripper is a person who is doing the best she can with the assets she has to make money and provide for her family, and I respect that — mostly her assets. Basically, I do not go simply because I am too cheap to enjoy a strip club, and I do not view such as a spectator sport.

As for the Georgia Tech grad, it sounds like he got a master's in finance that night for $53,000. Welcome to the real world, buddy boy! Too bad that, in your mid-twenties, your dad is still fighting your battles. There is a job waiting for you in a government procurement office.

Pain is an excellent teacher, and often in a society that makes excuses for bad behavior, it can be the only teacher. Of course, ridicule helps, which is what I do. It is my way of giving back. I am, if nothing else, a giver.

The dad, in playing the victim card here, is funny to me. Poor kid! The stripper and seedy club owner took the money he signed for. The 24-

year-old must be devastated. Who can he trust after that experience? Not even Oprah would take up his cause on this one.

Experiences are life's lessons through which certain harsh truths are conveyed to us Homo sapiens — and straight sapiens, too. I would like to think that our education system would teach them, but I have long ago given up on government-run schools.

Leave it to a stripper to teach this boy and others one of the most valuable lessons of life: Don't be an idiot. Everyone has a role in our society, even strippers.

One Tequila, Two Tequila, Three Tequila — Floor

"I have taken more out of alcohol than alcohol has taken out of me."

— Winston Churchill

Our kids can go to Iraq at eighteen but cannot drink until they are twenty-one. The law is plain in its language: it is twenty-one to drink, no matter if you are an Eagle Scout or a Kennedy. This got me thinking about drinking and who should and should not drink.

Now I have been in about 100 business deals in my lifetime, and got completely cheated two times — both by holier-than-thou men who did not drink. So I would agree with W.C. Fields when he said, "Never trust a man who does not drink." But there are degrees of drinking, and everyone, in time, gets to know their own. Not knowing your limits makes you a bad drunk, and no one wants to be a bad drunk.

I am told by a reliable source that "The Fuhrer," Adolph Hitler, did not like to drink tequila. He confided in a close friend that it just made him mean.

Personally, I do like to have a drink from time to time, (that time being after five p.m. and all weekend.) But thank goodness I get hangovers, so I do limit myself; I never drive after drinking — anymore. Drinking has been in my blood for years. The VD is new, but drinking has been there awhile.

Thinking back on what I once did makes me cringe today. And I was considered a "good kid." My fraternity brothers should all be in jail now for the way they acted. Kids are a lot smarter about that than we were, and that is a very good thing.

I am also getting to the age when we know who the alcoholics are. Sad thing is that they often do not know who they are. Many friends have recognized they have a drinking problem and have "taken the cure," as a buddy of mine calls it. They go to drunk camp and hang around other drunks for weeks — with nothing to drink. That has to be painful for them and punishment enough for being a bad drunk. One friend said he was a drunk, not an alcoholic, so he did not have to attend meetings. Another said he thought about joining AA but heard they had a strict non-drinking policy.

Personally, I really cannot determine for another person if he or she is an alcoholic. I have heard someone refer to another person as an alcoholic who drank just as much as the guy he was talking about. Usually when you hide it or are in denial, you probably have a problem.

At the end of the day, if you hurt other people (or yourself) with your drinking then you should not drink. Or, heeding the words of Sir Winston Churchill, if alcohol takes more out of you than you get from it, then you should not drink. Your friends should support you in that.

The issue of drinking for some becomes a moral one. Most preachers today rail against drinking as a sin; but I have consulted clergy and educated people (mostly in bars) and determined that it is not in the Bible not to drink. Alcohol is not against the law, so the Bible would not call it a sin to drink. However, there are many ministers who preach that consumption of alcohol is a mortal sin. Sloth and envy are mortal sins, so I guess one should avoid being a lazy drunk, or wanting other peoples' stuff when you are drunk (otherwise known as being Democrats), but just drinking is not a sin.

This stems from a sincere, but in some ways hypocritical, desire to live righteous lives before God, as many people just make bad decisions while drunk. Rather, they make the decisions that they really want to make and blame it on the booze. Part of the reason I like to have a drink with folks is that I think it helps reveal who they really are. Like playing golf, it reveals someone.

There is no question that the Bible labels drunkenness (we call it alcoholism today) as a sin. Paul states that those who live a "partying" type of lifestyle will not enter Heaven. So Paris Hilton is out, which is probably no shock to anyone. In a jailhouse interview, Paris recently stated, "God has given her a second chance." Today, a spokesman for God denied he said that.

At the same time, neither Paul nor anyone in the Bible commands Christians to abstain from alcohol as a prerequisite for, or evidence of, salvation. Quite the contrary, he encourages bishops in the church to abstain from wine but suggests that others simply not be "given too much wine" (Titus 2:3).

And all my favorite and respected leaders from history drank. Many were accomplished drunks: Churchill, Jefferson, Franklin, Babe Ruth, and Reagan. Hitler (contrary to my pithy aforementioned tequila joke), Bill Clinton, Saddam Hussein, Madonna, and Osama bin Laden are non-drinkers. I wish George Bush would get back to drinking a bit; it might turn things around for him — and us. He cannot make any worse decisions than he has sober.

Stop Protecting Stupid People

*"You can't escape the responsibility of tomorrow
by evading it today."*

— Abe Lincoln

An alert reader from the Peoples Republic of Massachusetts sent me a piece about elected officials there contemplating requiring helmets for kids who play soccer. People send me these silly PC news items just to stir me up, much like they tap on the gorilla cage at the zoo in hopes of getting a reaction. It works.

State Representative Deborah Blumer, D-Framington, proposed that all Massachusetts soccer players be required to wear a helmet during games. My suggestion is for soccer players, whose hands are free by the rules of the game, use them to slap this lawmaker in the head.

It makes me think of how we tend to live in a world where legislators are still trying to make silly laws and interfere where they have no business. I wonder what has become of personal responsibility, consequences, and common sense. If people are not allowed to think for themselves, take measured risks, and accept the consequences, what kind of world will we have?

We are a nation that actually tries to blame others for us being fat. Thank goodness the government is there to protect us from ourselves by requiring food companies to label their products either no-fat, low-fat, or fat, but with a great personality. Even to be more PC since their spokesman was Southerner Colonel Sanders, Kentucky Fried Chicken has changed its name to KFC. They probably did this because their customers got winded saying the full name.

When we were kids we were living proof of "Survival of the Fittest." Our parents smoked in the car and kept the windows rolled up while doing so as we (without seat belts) climbed around in the back seat. We hitchhiked, rode in the backs of trucks, drank water from garden hoses, had BB gun fights, and played ball in our yards until dark.

Little League had tryouts, and not everyone made the team. We knew that and became better at baseball in order to make the team. We did not give ninth place ribbons and a trophy to anyone who just participated. It is not reasonable or healthy to rely on others to make you feel good about yourself. Kids who are propped up by the "feel good" nurturing of the liberal education establishment do not do well with the harsh realities of the business world.

Our parents never bailed us out of trouble with teachers or police. In fact, mine actually sided with the authorities when I got in trouble. And they were right: I did it. Yet we knew the good guys from the bad, the good "scoundrels" from the ones who were really trouble. We learned this through personal interaction, not the instant messaging/text message world of today. No one was able to reach us at all times of the day; now that seems like a dream. We had friends, we met them outside, and we played. Dinner was on the table when we got home, and we ate it with our family.

There is a great old joke that goes: "What does every redneck say before he dies? 'Hey fellers, watch this!'" Certainly we do stupid things, but the really stupid folks die from it. This greatly cuts down on the idiots whom we are going to have to support someday anyway. Darwin called it "Natural Selection" and "Survival of the Fittest."

I have scars from motorcycle accidents and football injuries, and I still limp a bit. I never thought to sue anyone over my injuries, nor have I ever talked to a shrink about them. And I have determined that my guy friends now all have the same pains for similar reasons. It is just what we are about. These guys are the successful risk takers, problem solvers, entrepreneurs and creative people who shape our world, not the whiners seeking contrived adulation.

When I interviewed for a job on Wall Street, it was hard to differentiate all the MBAs who wanted these elite jobs. Without even looking up from my résumé, one interviewer said to me, "Well, Mr. Hart, we see so many Ivy League MBAs here at Goldman Sachs; how are you different?" I thought for a second and said, "I have been to a cock fight, I have spent a night in a county jail, and I have seen a man bite another man's ear lobe off in a bar fight. Other than that, there is probably no difference."

This guy was shocked, and as my interviews went on that day each person would ask me in detail about that earlier comment. My thinking, and eventually theirs, was that we are all products of our experiences, and the ones that do not kill you make you stronger.

We all must take some risks, understand those risks and find a way to survive them. Failure, success, consequences, and the underlying premise of all human activity is that you, not the government or your parents, are responsible for yourself.

Generation Y-ners

You know it was a big news week when both Greta Van Susteren and Nancy Grace relocated from Aruba, where they were investigating the disappearance of Natalee Holloway, to Blacksburg, Virginia.

With all the media hysteria and second-guessing in the wake of the Virginia Tech shootings, there have been common threads running through it all. It is that somehow this college-aged group of young people, whom the media have dubbed "Generation Y" because they followed "Generation X" (and the media is nothing if not linear), has endured a great deal in their short lifetimes. I heard one psychologist talking head on TV whine that this poor Generation Y has had to live through Katrina, 9-11, and now the Virginia Tech shootings. She did so as if they somehow were heroes for having had to watch all that on TV. Poor kids who had to look up from killing people on their Xbox video games to see such things; it has to be hard on them.

Let's be clear about something. We as a nation are soft and getting softer with each generation. These kids have it better than any preceding generation. This generation is made to feel like victims by mainstream media and politicians who have set new speed records in politicizing this tragedy.

We need the Generation Y kids to not blame others and take a look at themselves. It is in their violent video games and movies that this shooter found inspiration. It is the reinforced mindset that life's slights and bumps are so devastating that such actions are somehow society's fault.

We do not need another gun control law, we need media self-control laws.

The political knee-jerk reaction here is to put another unenforceable law on the books, purportedly to keep something like this from happening again. These "new gun laws" will not affect anyone but us law-abiding citizens. The reasoning of the gun control people is that if they just require one more question on the form to get a gun, they might prevent something like this. And as we all intuitively know, someone buying a gun to commit murder would never risk not being completely honest on a form he had to fill out. Those retail store forms are something a mass murderer would never monkey with!

It is a best-case outcome for me that this Virginia Tech shooter killed himself, but sadly, thirty-two people too late. I wonder just how much different an outcome there might have been if one of these "men on campus" had acted like a man and stepped up at some point to fight this five-foot-nothing Asian kid. I wonder, too, that if this had happened in the real South, what the likelihood would be that one of my Skoal-dipping brethren might have had a gun or at least a can of whoop-ass that would have saved many lives. Lastly, I wonder if the politically correct crowd on America's campuses perhaps did not act here or during 9/11, as they were afraid they might offend a minority. The only person who tried to stop the gunman was a seventy-six-year-old Holocaust survivor. Talk about the greatest generation!

Imagine what a waste of time it would be for the Virginia Tech shooter to wait twenty years on death row, supported by taxpayer-funded lawyers. (The Brian Nichols courthouse shooter case in Atlanta, caught on tape, cost us more than one million dollars). Imagine, too, how hard the trial would be for the students' parents.

CBS fired radio-show host Don Imus over a tasteless, yet free-speech-protected, comment. At the same time, NBC rushed to air the lunatic rantings and musings the Virginia Tech murderer-terrorist sent to them, as he knew they would. But let me remind you, this is the same NBC that decided not to televise a crazy fan who ran on the field during one of its sporting broadcasts, citing fear of future "copy-cat" type antics. Wow, I wonder where the Virginia Tech shooter got his flair for the dramatic and why he sent his political ranting to this network?

It is time that we stop whining in America and blaming ourselves for everything the world wants to pin on us. People all over the world wake up in war-torn poverty, with no freedom, no means to make a living, no Wal-Mart to buy basic goods at great prices, no running water, medical care, or even schools. These Generation Y whiners and their facilitators in the media and academia need to be slapped and told to wake up. You won the lottery of life. Stop your complaining and go out there and make the best of it. As John Wayne said, "Life is tough, but it's tougher when you're stupid." Where are this generation's John Waynes?

It's Good to Be Us

"The New York Times, America's most venerated journal of treason reduced its paper size from 13 and a half inches to 12. I have not seen that much liberal shrinkage since John Kerry went windsurfing"

— Stephen Colbert

In a recent Harris poll that comes as a surprise to the mainstream media, 94 percent of Americans said that they are satisfied with their lives. The poll, which asked 1,000 people to rate their overall "satisfaction" level, found that the number who said they were either very or somewhat satisfied with their lot was up four percentage points from just two years ago.

Not surprisingly, Southerners were happier with their lives than New Yorkers and other Eastern residents. Of course, I read this poll in something other than my local monopoly paper or *The New York Times*. I'll admit it: I get *The Times* and skim it, so that neither you nor President Bush has to. President Bush has been heroic with his ongoing struggles with literacy.

This good news may seem incongruous with all the negative news that you read in most papers. It will take a Democratic President for *The Times* to start printing positive stories about the U.S. again. I am not surprised at this poll or that *The New York Times* ignored it. The news in *The Times* and most large monopoly liberal newspapers is so negative it would be hard to be very happy after reading it. The paper has this ability to have a story about rampant poverty in Darfur juxtaposed with an ad for $1,400 Gucci shoes on sale at Saks Fifth Avenue. Perhaps the hungry in Darfur can feast on the hypocrisy of our media.

Clearly, *The Times'* motto should be: "All the negative news fit to print — and a heaping helping of second guessing on the side." Carrying a positive story about the United States would contradict its main theme: This country stinks and it is the fault of the Republicans and dumb Southerners. No wonder circulation is dropping. I predict trouble for them as they continue to disenfranchise Americans with their nakedly ambitious liberal agenda.

They even had to dig up a story on Thomas Jefferson that he had affairs with his slaves and others. You'd think Jefferson was getting comfortable having covered up these affairs for 225 years and then bam, here comes *The New York Times* dishing dirt on one of our Founding Fathers. Is nothing off limits? Only NBA players are going to regret the discovery of DNA paternity test results more than past presidents.

Yet Americans only rank 112th in the happiest countries world rankings. If *The New York Times* folds, I bet we would move up to number 10.

What I miss about Ronald Reagan, besides his spending vetoes, was his optimism. Along with his belief in the individual and our ability to triumph over any adversity, Reagan gave us a contagious confidence. I believe in this strongly, yet I do not see our media or even our politicians today reinforcing this or the fundamental goodness of people.

This is a great time to be an American. And if you do not like today, tomorrow will be better. Even with 20 percent of our country defined as poor, only six percent are not satisfied with their lives. In America, even our poor people are fat and would make a nice middle class almost any-where else. While we whine and belittle ourselves, the inhabitants of many Third World countries are just hoping that one of our planes flies over and drops them a bag of rice grown and paid for by the industrious Americans they are conditioned to hate.

Our biggest concern is that everyone cannot afford a flat-screen TV. And if you cannot afford it today, look at Wal-Mart next month and the prices will be lower. Capitalism has done more for the well-being of Americans than any politician or editorial board ever has. You can bet that the nutcase terrorists who strap bombs on themselves to kill innocent people would not do that if they had career prospects.

I think our first, best export should be free trade capitalism, not democ-racy as Bush has tried. When capitalism takes hold, democracy follows.

So let's quickly counter the two fears that the "drive-by media" are pimping now: Iraq and global warming. First, we are not going to be defeated by a country that does not have food, electricity, or cable TV yet. Once they get cable, they will be too busy catching up on *Baywatch* to want to fight. Once they get that all worked out, we might worry that they can whoop us.

And if there is global warming, let me explain it. Go stand barefooted in your yard, then step on your driveway. Now relax, life is good.

Justice is Not Only Blind, It Must Be Drunk Too

Justice is a machine that, when someone has given it a starting push, rolls on of itself."

— John Galsworthy

It seems the liberals who idolize those who marched for causes du jour in the 1960s are digging hard to find injustices in America against which they can march today. The worst thing about them protest marching is that, after getting drunk on one apple martini, they tell people about it for the next fifty years.

In fact, I would argue that there is so much justice in America today we need to back it off a touch. Every half-baked group that shows up at any event will get news cameras there to cover them if it fits into the media's liberal agenda. They just call themselves "The concerned this and thats," and if it fits the media's view of the world, they get airtime.

I would like to live in a town that could actually be depended on to convict O.J. Simpson, Robert Blake, Marion Barry, and Phil Spector. That, to my way of thinking, would be a good litmus test as to whether the town had any sense at all. I am looking at you, L.A., where reasonable doubt is defined as the jury recognizing you as a celebrity.

The problem with letting guilty folks go is that they will do it again. O.J. was in Las Vegas, speaking, I believe, at a double-murderers convention, when he and some of the quality individuals he hangs out with decided to rob a guy at gunpoint. People actually marched in favor of O.J., and news cameras were there. I think they were the same people in the Michael

Moore documentaries. O.J. might skate on this one too, since the victim has said that he will not press charges in return for O.J. not murdering him.

In fact, there is so much media attention at an O.J. trial that Las Vegas should be in for a nice economic boom. I have asked the Atlanta major to put together a nice bid for our city to host the next O.J. trial. It is between us and Detroit, insiders say.

Then there is the case of the Atlanta courthouse murderer, Brian Nichols. Imprisoned for a brutal rape, the former college football player took a gun from the five-foot, two-inch tall, fifty-one-year old female sheriff's deputy who was assigned to escort him — in another nice win for women's equality in the workforce, as well as another blow to common sense — and shot and killed the judge, bailiff, court reporter, and a Customs agent. Much of this took place in front of cameras, and the prosecution has 400 witnesses.

It makes me long for the days when such evil people as Brian Nichols were found shot fifty-five times and the local sheriff proclaims it to be "the most comprehensive suicide he had ever seen."

There are two liberal knee-jerk reactions to a murderous shooting-spree like this one. First, they want to take guns away from the people who did not do the crime. And second, they spend unlimited amounts of taxpayer money to defend and try to understand the murderer.

Instead of frying this guy within a week, he has been allowed to have four attorneys, paid for by my tax dollars, who have run up a $1.8 million legal tab defending him. Now I am not sure what Perry Mason-like magic these low-life attorneys who have the gall to represent Brian Nichols are planning to put forth at trial, but I am sure that at least one of them has a ponytail and advertises on a bus.

If you take a defense job like this as an attorney, you do it for two reasons. One, you want to look like an edgy champion of justice, which will get you laid by Goth chicks with multiple tattoos. Secondly, you could not get by in the private sector where people actually spend their own money. So you run up a big legal bill, and sadly, our government allows it. Justice is not only blind; it must be drunk, too.

Nichols was captured after he fled to suburban Atlanta where he held Ashley Smith captive in her apartment. She had walked outside for a smoke, and he accosted her (yet another reason not to smoke, kids). He asked her for some pot. She was not prepared for guests, and could only offer him her personal meth.

But she did read to Nichols from the Bible and *The Purpose-Driven Life*, which, along with the meth, calmed him. My guess is that his defense attorneys will say that his constitutional rights were violated, which prohibits him from having to hear any reference to God for any reason in public. The trampling of Brian Nichols' constitutional rights lasted into the night, and the next morning she made him pancakes for breakfast, then sneaked out and called 911. This is certainly a case where a religious crystal-meth user had an advantage over a non-addict atheist. Reading Christopher Hitchen's *God is Not Great: How Religion Poisons Everything* to Nichols would not have had the same outcome unless he was a book reviewer for *The New York Times*.

Justice is no doubt a noble pursuit, but more a virtuous one is sensible stewardship of public money. If we keep wasting money like this, we will be broke and then even the simple administration of justice will not be possible.

Internet Dating and Other Oxymorons

"A man is seldom better than his conversation."

— German Proverb

The Internet has brought with it much joy and heartache since Al Gore single-handedly created it (in his mind), before he made up the scary global warming stuff. Both kids and adults have had their interpersonal skills either heightened or dulled by the Internet.

My parents recently lost a friend to the Internet's reach. Their seventy-one-year-old next-door neighbor was able to reconnect with his high school girlfriend once he finally learned to use his dial-up connection. After finding her on Classmates.com and e-mailing her for two years, he came in one day and announced to his wife of forty-five years that he was leaving her. My parents told me of this with sadness, and my response was that they should look at the bright side; it would have been sooner if he had sprung for DSL.

I wonder what the net effect of getting to know each other via virtual communication will be on teenagers. In my day we awkwardly learned about sex the old-fashioned way — through trial and error, mostly the latter in my case.

On that note, I would like to take this opportunity to officially and publicly apologize to the first five women I dated. It had to have been a terrible experience and for that, I am very sorry. Liquored up and in the back seat of a Monte Carlo with a landau roof is no way to have your first romantic experience. I understand that now.

Back then we had dates. We actually went out, we talked, and we later married one of them — either by choice or because she was pregnant. If there is a bright spot today, it is that fewer girls are getting impregnated by idiot guys. This remarkable trend, however, may have been reversed recently by Kevin Federline.

My first date in a small town was like something out of a sitcom. There were a lot of reasons a girl would not go out with me, chief among them being that my scrawny and bow-legged appeal was very limited. Imagine Napoleon Dynamite without the nunchucks skills, cool clothes, or the ability to dance. Around my sophomore year I was starting to play my cards right with the ladies. Up until that point, I had played a lot of solitaire.

That was when I finally did find a girl who would be my beta test for dating. I set my goals low and continued to lower them until this one girl went out with me. There are a couple of things you would never hear this girl say, one of which was, "I will not go out with him," and the other probably was "checkmate."

It is a wonderful thing when a young male's inhibitions and standards are lowered to that optimal level to find a date. I would like to mention her name, but I have been admonished by her attorneys not to ever publicly identify her.

So, unlike kids today, I got dressed up and picked her up for a nice dinner out. I cannot recall exactly when or why I decided that a plaid suit with eight-inch lapels would be a good choice for the first date, but pictures taken at the time have well documented my haute couture atrocity.

We went to the nicest place in my town, which seemingly was where everyone who had a sports coat was that night. We may or may not have had some Blue Nun wine that I scored, but we did dance to the strains of a $150 band's rendition of "China Grove."

She admittedly did not like me at first, but I sensed that, over time, she developed a tolerant indifference towards me. But we had trust issues. We eventually broke up when I caught her lying — under another guy at a bonfire.

We had a terrific time dating, which leads me to wonder how differently my interpersonal skills would have developed if the Internet had existed back then, or whether I would have developed any interpersonal skills at all. I would not have bothered to date, given the "virtual dating" opportunities the Internet presents to a young male.

Kids today seem to be mortified to actually have personal contact with another of their species. Instead of face-to-face encounters, many devote hours instead to developing personal websites on social networking sites, where they reveal dangerous personal information that they would never share with someone in person. Long-term, this cannot be healthy.

And for all of us, with or without the Internet, youth is an awkward time. I just question how technology will affect this generation.

Even with the Internet being our dating service, once women and men get into a relationship it remains difficult. Women hold on to the antiquated notion that sex and love are somehow related. Women often fake orgasms for the sake of a relationship. And men will always fake a relationship for the sake of an orgasm. We call this a "relationship," and it can work for years this way.

Love and romance are one of the most written-about subjects in America today, yet they are less and less practiced in a world of impersonal Internet and text message communications. This is the reason to preserve the old black-and-white movies of Bogie and Bacall and the like. Soon, the classic love stories will be the how-to guide in the documentary section of your Blockbuster store.

Working Harder Than A Rented Mule

"My favorite animal is the mule. He has a lot more horse sense than a horse. He knows when to stop eating. And he knows when to stop working."

— Harry S. Truman

Spring has always been my favorite time of year. As the weather begins to warm up, so does the NCAA basketball tournament (my Tigers are in again), the Masters, and Mule Day. Two of the three events get plenty of press, so let me tell you about my hometown's annual Mule Day event.

Columbia, Tennessee has been celebrating the mule and our historic relationship with this hard-working and ornery animal every spring since 1840 — well before I was in a position to get kicked by one. And considering we are located next to Pulaski, where the Ku Klux Klan was founded, and near Carthage, where Al Gore was born, I always reasoned that Mule Day was not a bad historic event to celebrate.

Columbia is, after all, the "the Mule Capital of the World." Not just the United States, the world! Take that Winfield, Alabama! So this is not a nickel-and-dime operation. Back before tractors, the engine, garden tillers, and illegal aliens, mules were the working real deal, worthy of celebration.

The event has a mule-pulling contest, knife and coin show, square dancing, cowboy-mounted shooting contest, and a lumberjack exhibition (which I think is a subtle reach out to the lesbian community). There is also an amateur liars contest, which the many politicians who attend the event are forbidden to enter since they are professionals.

Two experiences come to mind as I think back on the Mule Days of my youth. One of the guys on our football team, a third-year junior, got thrown out of the festival once for heckling a mule. I wanted to see it go on longer as it was a very evenly matched intellectual contest.

A better memory is that I once dated a Mule Day Queen. It was, and is, a big deal to win that title in my hometown. It was not until a year later, away at college, when I was bragging at the SAE house about dating the Mule Day Queen that I realized the story did not travel well.

What I learned about mules in my upbringing has served me well in dealing with people. I learned to never try to teach a mule to think or reason. It just does not work, and it just annoys the mule — all the while making you look stupid for even trying (see football player above).

You never want to get yourself in a position where you are matching wits with a far inferior intellectual creature. It is the same reason no one should strike up a conversation with a liberal Democrat at a bar. Reasoning with them is harder than hitting a wiffle ball to right field.

What you have to love about mules and all animals is that they always seem to enjoy the moment. Only man seems to worry about things. Animals know that the primary principle of life is to enjoy it. And they never seem to pass any judgment or ask many questions of others — an admirable trait.

Mule Day is so big that I even saw a picture of it on the front page of *The New York Times*. Oddly enough, the article was not what I expected, a chance for the snooty *Times* to belittle Southern traditions. Rather, it was about the allocation of Homeland Security money to the event. I take issue with that. The terrorists who so value their camels would like nothing more than to attack our national mule stockpile. That many mules all gathered in one place would be too enticing to al-Qaeda and to one odd guy in our town named Clyde.

Al-Qaeda terrorists could not move so freely in the Mule Day crowd and they would be easy to detect. And what with all the guns and knives around, wielded by local owner-operators of same, the terrorists would not have the upper hand. I am just glad the U.S. government was there to protect us.

This year's Mule Day is the April 2nd weekend, with Vols ex-coach Phil Fulmer as Grand Marshall. Get there before he eats all the hot dogs. If you would like to see a true slice of Americana, attend!

Bonnaroo: Been There, Done That, Bought a T-shirt

Ron and his son Jeb at Bonnaroo — with the T-shirt

Last week I attended the Bonnaroo Music and Arts Festival, courtesy of the Manchester, Tennessee paper that carries my column. They even got me a VIP pass, so as not to miss the opportunity to raise the median age of the attendees by at least twenty years.

Bonnaroo is an amazing series of concerts on a 700-acre farm between Nashville and Chattanooga. It is like an annual Woodstock, where modern-day hippies and hipsters camp, and watch top bands play for four days. I did not camp, however. As I came to discover, camping involves the outdoors, and I do not like discomfort in any form. The outdoors is best left there.

I was initially told that Bonnaroo is a made-up word that means nothing, just like "Lollapalooza" or "congressional ethics." Later, I found out that it is Cajun slang for "fun."

There were mostly kids with nose rings and tattoos wearing bathing suits they really should have reconsidered. In fact, although I am steadfastly against more government, I really think some of these women need to apply for a permit to wear a two-piece. Bill Clinton could chair the committee to review applicants; he'd like that.

One person died and I am sure countless kids had to be untangled from making out with other joyful souls with nose rings. More STDs were passed around than during Paris Hilton's last night out before prison. I bet right now numerous attendees are checking their crotches just hoping that is only a bug bite.

As you might imagine, the Birkenstock crowd there had all their liberal causes. Kids seemed more interested in the world's problems than any solutions. As best I can figure, they like to "raise awareness" in hopes that someone else will actually do something about it — perhaps their parents who paid for their $250 ticket. It also is apparently nobler to be an activist in non-quantifiable things on a grand scale, such as world pollution and the environment. That is easier than actually showering and cleaning up their campsites. And chicks dig it.

Yet again, the entrepreneurial spirit abounded, a shining example of the same capitalism that they seem to detest on a larger scale. Vendors offered a wide array of pot, coke, and acid for a reasonable market-driven price. Ironically, drugs were sold at a more competitive price than the prescription drug benefit Congress "gave" us, because at least at Bonnaroo, the drug dealers are forced to compete.

The way dealers at Bonnaroo operate is that when they walk past someone, they say the name of their product. So I hear the word "pot" said by a passerby. If you wanted to buy said product, then, unlike our government's drug purchases, you would engage a vendor in price negotiations. And like most all of my purchases, they would begin with, "You ain't no cop, right?"

Being one of the oldest dudes there, I really did not get many offers to "Rock the Vote" or buy drugs. In fact, I am not sure that when I walked by one dealer, he did not say "Geritol."

They register voters there because they know they are going to vote for Democrats, since they get most of their political views from the drummer for Third Eye Blind. The same drummer who rails against oil companies'

10-cent-a gallon profit has no problem selling his band's T-shirts at his concert for $35.

Another barker said that he was for Hillary Clinton because she would fight global warming. I told him that he might be onto something; there is nothing about Hillary that is warm, so she really cannot be the least bit to blame for that.

Another "activist" told me he was going to vote for Dennis (the Munchkin) Kucinich because of his strong environmental stance. He kept citing the talking points to me, such as some scientists say the oceans will rise four feet because of global warming. This made me understand why Kucinich is fighting that so much, since he would probably drown.

All in all, I really enjoyed Bonnaroo. I would advise all of the forty-some-things to try it. On one hand, it makes one feel old. Yet, with the vibrancy and infectious, carefree atmosphere, it makes you feel young and rejuvenated. And it reminds us that, although getting old is inevitable, acting old is optional.

My Colonoscopy: Where No Man Has Gone Before

This week my doctor went boldly where no man has gone before by conducting my first colonoscopy. I gravitate toward doctors who play golf, especially those who putt well because their hands do not shake.

The procedure went well, but now I know how those sock puppets in the media feel. For Wolf Blitzer's sake, I hope David Axelrod has small hands. I have no regrets about doing this, except that I hate to do that on the first date — but he was "a doctor." I just hope he calls me again.

Turning 50 this year made it my time to ride the silver rocket. "Proctologist" is a word a straight man never likes to hear, along with a few others like "testicular," "ingrown," "listen," "ask for directions," and "let's cuddle." But I knew the colonoscopy was something I had to do, and you should, too.

First, they make you stop eating the day before and drink a particularly obnoxious concoction called "MoviPrep."

This stuff can only be described as tasting like tinsel from your Christmas tree ground up into creek water coming from near a phosphate plant. I think they do that so you cannot take a plane out of town; you would not get through a TSA metal detector.

In about thirty minutes you understand what the "Mov" part of MoviPrep means. Not to be indelicate, but you run to your potty, and you and the toilet make like a jet ski for the next hour. It is like that scene from the movie *Dumb and Dumber.* You know the one, done back when

Jim Carrey was funny and not trying to get an Oscar.

If Obama would just allow it, they should use MoviPrep on captured al-Qaida fighters. After taking it, everything comes out. It is like a divorcee after three vodkas at Houston's.

Then a loved one, or someone just looking for entertainment, drives you to the procedure. You meet with the anesthesiologist, who, by American Medical Association rules, has to be foreign. You then impart critical personal information to this person, who is going to put you to as near to death as you have yet come. Can you think of a better time to have communication difficulties?

They roll you into a room and put an IV in your arm in preparation for putting you into a mini-sleep — or, as Michael Jackson called it, "afternoon nap time." I woke up about an hour later thinking I was in a scene from *Slum Dog Millionaire*, but it was just the anesthesiologist asking me questions.

Once you can stand up, they release you to go home. Come to think of it, that's the same thing my local bartender does. I saw a Candy Striper on the way out of the procedure room and really hoped it was not Richard Simmons.

You feel a bit groggy and have an eerie feeling that you may have fallen asleep in a gay bar. Not that I ever have — again. They say you cannot drive that day or my favorite, "operate heavy machinery." This conveniently fits my lifelong rule: Do Not Operate Heavy Machinery — EVER. I actually call office staff in to operate my stapler.

I hope this answers your questions about getting a colonoscopy. And to you liberal bloggers out there, the answer is "no." My doctor did not find my head up there.

It was a lot less traumatic than my guy friends had taunted. The good news is that since it went well, I do not have to have another one for ten years.

So, when Obama's health care bill gets passed this year, I am going to immediately fill out the necessary eighty pages of federal paperwork and apply to the Colonoscopy Czar of the Amalgamated Service Workers Union Local 1984 for my next one in 2019.

God, I hope the feds do not read my columns.

Small-Town Boy Proves There is Goodness in Golf

I often get accused of playing too much golf, a game I dearly love. That's a fair enough charge, especially coming from my historically golf-tolerant wife, who recently told me that I "loved golf more than her." Having been told by psychologists, clergy, and the like to never deny a woman her feelings and to always say something positive, I simply responded that it may be true, but "I love you more than hockey."

That said, I would not trade anything for my golf-related experiences. The friendships I have enjoyed and the lessons I have learned have had a profound impact on my business, personal life, and family life.

Golf, once viewed as an elitist sport, has become more egalitarian. We avidly cheer the success of stellar golfers like Tiger Woods and Vijay Singh, who succeed not by the color of their skin but through hard work and talent. To this point, I will relay this inspiring story that a friend whose son competes in high school golf told me last week.

Near my Tennessee hometown is Madison, a small city near Nashville. Joe David, a kid from that unlikely town, recently won the state high school golf championship, a title usually won by golfers from powerhouse schools like Baylor in Chattanooga.

Joe had a difficult upbringing. His dad was not around, and his mom wrestled with addictions. Nevertheless, like a family should do, someone stepped up and took responsibility for Joe at a young age. In this case it was his grandfather, Woody Keen, a hard-working house painter. Life was tough for the family, but they were determined to prove themselves tougher.

Seeing that young Joe had an interest in golf, his grandfather sought to help him as best he could. He worked a deal with a local golf course to paint its clubhouse if the club would allow his grandson to play golf there.

Golf became Joe's escape; it's hard to remember how difficult a place the world can be when one plays golf.

As Joe's talent was revealed, he was afforded the opportunity to opt out of the government-run school system and was able, with the financial help of his grandfather, to attend the private Goodpasture High School. Joe felt then that he could do anything, except of course dance, as Goodpasture is a Church of Christ school. There he got the support and instruction he needed to excel, soon winning many junior titles.

The crowning achievement was when he won the Tennessee high school golf title. On November 14, the family will be rewarded when Joe signs a scholarship to play college golf for Ole Miss.

Whether he plays professional golf or not, Joe has been revealed to the world as a class act. When he won the Jerry Cole Sportsmanship Award, he humbly said, "I do not know if I can ever repay the game of golf for all it has done for me."

Fundamental to all real golfers is a sense of fair play and respect for honest work. We know the simple truth that as we work toward climbing a mountain, most of the happiness and personal growth occur during the climb. Joe's grandfather set the tone with his sacrifices that inspired Joe to work hard at this game of golf, which many say is the sport that comes closest to mirroring life. Further, what we relearn through a story like Joe David's is that some of the best teachers in the world are caring grandparents.

Taking to heart the idea that the lasting legacy of any adult should be to reach out and help someone when he or she can are visionaries like Jack Lupton. Lupton, through his famed Honors Course, long ago realized that the amateur is the heart and soul of golf, and he has funded and recognized kids like Joe David for more than twenty years. Many caddies, aspiring high school golfers, and the like have been given scholarships through the benevolence of Jack and golfers everywhere.

In the demands it places on the individual, golf invites only those willing to step up to the never-ending challenge. They understand that the lasting lessons taught in golf, even if it is not played at the highest level, endure a lifetime. Golf is an honorable game that has no referees and does not change its rules to attract fans. Golfers do not shoot up nightclubs when they visit a town. Their venues are not taxpayer-funded, and they actually raise money for local charities and leave the town better than they found it.

Golfers like Joe David and thousands of others are the reasons the game means so much to so many of us.

Matt Ryan, Bill Gates, and Ron Hart at Augusta National Golf Club

Acknowledgements

Dear family and friends have been the riches of my life. There must be no greater trial than to be close to someone who has as many opinions as I have and the inability to suppress them. For those friendships, and for the laughs we have shared over the years, I thank the many people who have come into my life and so enhanced it. Whether you blame or congratulate them, my writing would not have come about without the encouragement and support of the following family and friends.

First, and because they make my life so much easier, I thank my family; you know who you are, especially since DNA tests have become so accurate. I kid and make fun of everyone I value in my life; it is just what straight guys do. It is our way of saying "I love you." If we say nothing, then we do not like you.

I owe special thanks to my friends who, at the risk of great personal ridicule, supplied blurbs for my book: Fred Barnes of Fox News, P.J. O'Rourke of P.J. O'Rourke fame, and Bob Johnson and Bernie Marcus, two of the most admired billionaire founders of companies in America and all-around great guys. And to Matt Ryan, Scott Kent, and Nick Gillespie, I appreciate you guys doing this.

Thanks to old high school friends Ed Lancaster, Emily McKnight, Ben McKnight, Barry Daniels, Joe Whitehead, Jimmy and Melinda Houston, Darrell Lynn, Greg Webb, Mike Vaughan, Bren Hardison, Delilah Riddle, Jim Ross, Dan West, Tad Mays, Sonny Shackelford, Joe Pinckney, the Flemings, and the McKays. I also send special thanks to Ulysses Crawley for not killing me in the locker room. We survived the public school system together. And thanks to Columbians Julie Gillen and Steve Rowland for their insights on my columns.

College friends I thank include John Farris; George Flanigen; Walker Taylor; Mike Thompson; The Horns; Turner Echols; the Scotts: Driver, Fleming, Kenney, and Lucas; Bruce Hillyer; Rob Joyner; Van Weinberg; Rob Preston; John Hughes; John Coates; and Bob Schriner.

I thank my buddies at Goldman Sachs for letting me hang out around much smarter people during my career, including my pal Barry Hines, Scott Lucas, Tom Albertson, Peter Mallinson, Rick Elfman, Scott Jenkins, Bobby Tudor, Mark Ordan, Mark Fife, Ken Dengler, Bill Gruver, Bob Dahl, Steve Heftner, David Windreich, Steve Tuttle, and Larry Levy.

Doctors Joyce Jensen, Don Carson, Jim Beaty, Seiler, Pepin, Grover, Lazar, Viksnins, and Mitchell round out the more educated folks I would like to thank. Their ability to encourage me and write prescriptions at the same time makes them indispensable.

Families from Florida, Tennessee, and Atlanta whose encouragement I am grateful for are the Astors, Henritzes, Davidsons, Sauls, Oehmigs, Gibsons, Curries, Kabus, Fuquas, FitzGeralds, Jacobsons, Shaws, Drymans, Montgomerys, Striblings, Buffingtons, Worthingtons, Steels, Eddys, Sugrues, Feidlers, Pendergastss, Drivers, Egans, Balls, Wynnes, Sheltons, Stevens, Hurds, Popes, Tompkins, Gows, Mannings, Jensens, Gaffneys, Hanuseks, and Grizzards. And a special thank-you to Frank Hanna, a paragon of intellectual reasoning. I also thank my ancestor, John Hart, for signing the Declaration of Independence.

I owe a debt of gratitude to the woefully underpaid purveyors of local sentiment who edit the papers in which my columns appear. I owe special thanks to the first newspaper editor to pick up my column, Chris Fletcher of the *Columbia Daily Herald*. Other editors who encouraged me and bravely ran my column early on include Scott Kent, William Hatfield, Sam Hatcher, Jim Bryan, Chip & Beth Ramsey, Sam Mitchell, Jimmy Espy, Linda Fudala, Jim Tucker, Len Labarth, Davis Sons, Barbara Shold, Ken Brodnax, Stan Mitchell and Jim Calicutt. Gwen Break, Debbie Wheeler, and Karen Hanes are to be thanked as well.

And to Boo Weekly, the bloggers, and those who email me ideas and thoughts that I often incorporate into columns, you guys are helpful.

Radio and TV friends who have been so kind to me include Martha Zoller, Josh Davis, Denny Schaffer, Henry Cho, Burnie Thompson, and especially a great American, Lee Sullivan of Panama City Beach, Florida.

I also thank all of the folks at CNN who have been so helpful. And, to my publisher, Jan Schroder of Schroder Publishing, Paul Holliday for the cartoons and Heidi Rizzi for design and layout of the book, thank you. You guys are the best.

Lastly, thank you to those who edited and taught me grammar at age 43, Miriam Stix, Marc Pelath, and Michelle Covert. Special thanks to Michelle — you are the best, Rock Chalk or not!

Emulating worthy role models is the only way one can strive to be better. I thank you all for the positive influence you have had in my life, and I look forward to many more laughs, debates, and special moments.